TREAT YOUR CUSTOMERS LIKE ANIMALS

T0362965

GLOBAL
PUBLISHING
G R O U P

Global Publishing Group
Australia • New Zealand • Singapore • America • London

TREAT YOUR CUSTOMERS
LIKE ANIMALS

THE COUNTERINTUITIVE GUIDE TO INCREASING SALES WITHOUT SELLING

JOHN S. MCKINSTRY

First Edition 2018

A copy of this publication can be found in the National Library of Australia.

John S McKinstry
Treat Your Customers Like Animals And Increase Your Sales By Twenty-Plus Percent Without Selling!

1st ed.
ISBN: 9781925288858 (pbk.)

 A catalogue record for this book is available from the National Library of Australia

Published by Global Publishing Group
PO Box 517 Mt Evelyn, Victoria 3796 Australia
Email Info@GlobalPublishingGroup.com.au

Printed in China

For further information about orders:
Phone: +61 3 9739 4686 or Fax +61 3 8648 6871

Acknowledgements

*To the **nem** Partners*

All of whom have contributed to shaping the VALUE Encounter Methodology that has been developed by the firm and is outlined in this book.

The core VALUES of the firm are enshrined in this approach which is driven by an overriding objective of assisting businesses to achieve their objectives far more quickly than they can on their own AND of only engaging when genuine value-added outcomes can be achieved.

As you will see this is not always as obvious as one would like but, as the firm has proven time and time again, every business holds hidden potential and identi-fying that together can be a rewarding and genuinely enjoyable process for all those involved.

Contents

Foreword

All the consulting engagements undertaken by **nem** are derived from referrals and the firm has worked with a wide range of referrers over the years; none more so than accounting firms.

To put the content of this book into context; when accountants network for new business in forums where they do not know too many people; when the question is asked '... and what is that you do?' and they respond '... I am an accountant', there is usually polite conversation for a short period of time before the person is distracted and moves on.

When we started our consulting firm and networked for new business in forums where we did not know too many people; when asked '... and what is it that you do?' and we responded'... I am a consultant' ... there was no conversation and the person quickly moved on. Clearly, we needed to develop a different approach, an approach that created conversation, engagement, and opened up commercial opportunities.

The approach we developed and successfully applied is called the VALUE Encounter Methodology and it is arguably one of the most effective soft skills business development frameworks to be developed and applied, and has particular relevance to professional services firms and the accounting profession.

This book outlines the journey of the firm and one of the founders' commercial experiences that shaped the **VALUE** Encounter methodology as it is applied today.

You will learn that nurturing your customers like animals, classifying them as Elephants, Tigers, Cats and Kittens and interacting with them according to their relationship, not according to their actual or perceived monetary value, will profoundly improve your businesses sales performance.

---

[1] Value Encounter® is a trademarked methodology of Non-Executive Management Services Pty Ltd.

CHAPTER 1

Introduction

CHAPTER 1

....

Introduction

The VALUE Encounter Methodology

The **VALUE** Encounter Methodology is a unique framework that ensures businesses obtain what they **WANT** by identifying what they **NEED** to do to obtain it. It sounds simple, but as you will see there are a myriad of biases, preconceived views and opinions, and a vast array of emotional and physical dynamics that preclude this simple objective from being consistently and reliably achieved.

The cornerstone to an effective **VALUE** Encounter, whether it's the engagement with prospective customers, networking to obtain new customers, or servicing the requirements of existing customers, is the relationship that you have with the party with whom you are communicating.

Not all relationships are the same, and not all customers are the same. Often when people operate in business they gravitate towards those individuals or organisations that they believe can help them the most, particularly when looking for new business opportunities or selling additional products and services to existing customers. This is a fundamentally flawed approach resulting in a significant waste of time and effort.

Relying solely on what we believe and what we know limits our opportunities. No one knows everything and everyone around us knows things which we do not. This extends to every person we know in our networks and within our customer portfolios. We just need to know how to unlock their potential.

If you look at your customers and prospects according to their actual or perceived monetary value to you or your organisation, or if look at your network and grade the usefulness of those that you know according to your commercial objectives, you probably adopt some form of traditional A, B, C and D grading criterion.

If this is the case, you will benefit significantly from learning how to treat your customers like animals, by classifying them as Elephants, Tigers, Cats and Kittens and interacting with them according to their status, not according to their actual or perceived monetary value.

As you will see, this approach is counterintuitive. It is revolutionary in terms of conventional business development techniques, is replicable and will rapidly increase your sales effectiveness.

Before you can apply this approach consistently and intuitively you need to understand the **VALUE** Encounter Methodology and the three cornerstones of its consistent application.

The *first cornerstone* is understanding the type of relationship you have with the party with whom you are interacting. The *second cornerstone* is securing engagement with those relationships. The *third cornerstone* is the delivery of value-added outcomes as a result of that engagement.

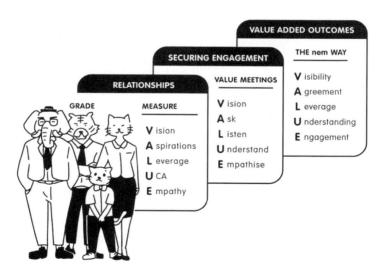

A common acronym, **VALUE**, is applied to each cornerstone but refers to the different tools and approaches that are used with each one.

As you will learn, the *first cornerstone* requires you to classify your clients (and networks) as animals and, where you know them well, to measure your knowledge of them with the **VALUE** Encounter measurement tool. This tool requires you to self-assess your knowledge of clients prior to meeting with them.

The *second cornerstone* requires you to undertake a **VALUE** Encounter meeting to confirm or complete your knowledge of them. These meetings vary according to the clients' animal classification, but are always focused on the other party and their business or personal objectives.

The *third cornerstone* requires you to deliver on the value-added opportunities that have been identified, by balancing what the clients **want** with what they **need** to do to obtain it. At **nem** we refer to this as 'The **nem** Way'. As you will see, **nem** has a proprietary review process that shares information, unlocks hidden potential and helps businesses to prioritise their actions, but there are numerous ways in which a business can achieve the same **VALUE**-added outcomes for their customers.

As you will learn, a **VALUE**-added outcome may not be the immediate sale of your product or service, although this will invariably occur with Tigers and Cats. It could be as simple as improving a client's opinion of you, elevating your status, widening each other's understanding of your respective objectives or building your relationship to referral status.

These three critical cornerstones emerged to make our approach truly unique. When we started to investigate the viability of establishing **nem**, they did not emerge clearly or in this order: the journey of discovery was one of trial and error, observation and collaboration.

Additionally, the critical elements of developing meaningful and commercially effective relationships within the framework were reinforced by a lifetime of business experience.

CHAPTER 2

The Beginning of nem

CHAPTER 2

....

The Beginning of nem

nem emerged from a desire to own and operate my own business. This is a common entrepreneurial trait that many corporate executives hold but rarely have the opportunity to explore, due to the demands of their employers and the loss of security that comes with 'going it alone'.

It should be no surprise that I was between roles when my desire became a genuine option that was worthy of thorough investigation. It soon became obvious that there was a correlation between the financial resources I could apply, or put at risk, and the size of the organisations that could present the opportunities and challenges I was looking for. This meant joining forces with others, leveraging more heavily, or taking on risky businesses; and eventually a loose group of acquaintances and I started evaluating many different businesses and looking into all aspects of their operations.

We quickly gained a healthy respect for the mainly private business owners and found ourselves contemplating purchases in industries in which we had little, if any, experience. This was fraught with danger, and after coming very close to buying into a power tool business we eventually had a meeting of the minds.

What did all the businesses we came across have in common? A committed and passionate owner! Yes – who was an expert in their core areas – but what else? None of them could see where their business needed assistance, and often this assistance was needed a long time before they decided they wanted to sell. They were all blind to underlying issues that impeded the optimum performance of their business – or, at a very minimum, that had prevented us from being prepared to acquire them.

As we contemplated our experiences over several months it became apparent that perhaps there was a real commercial opportunity in providing these businesses with the experience and assistance that they needed. The concept of **nem** (non-executive management) was born, and three of us agreed to examine this market opportunity thoroughly.

Those three were myself, Noel Scully and Andrew Jones. I had worked with Noel when he was the commercial manager of a group of manufacturing operations. We had kept in touch but were not best mates; we just had a healthy respect for one another. Noel was a few years younger than myself, an accountant by profession who had moved into general management. Andrew was twelve-odd years older than Noel and had worked in a wide range of senior executive roles. He had a science background in polymer technology and was extremely well connected in comparison with Noel and myself.

Everything is Referred

Our first revelation, supported by research and experience, was that every prospective client was more than likely going to be referred to us. That meant cold calling, slick marketing and clichés were not going to cut it. We needed to be *referred* to business owners, and the more reliable and trustworthy the referrer was, the better the quality of the referral or prospect.

Our research showed that the most reliable sources of advice to a business were the business owner's accountant, followed by friends, mentors and family, and then their bankers. The only group we knew was bankers, so that meant if we wanted referrals, we needed to be professional, maintain high ethics and respect the banker's relationship with their client above all else. This view and proposition led us to develop the first of three aspects of our approach that did, and still does, differentiate us from nearly every other consulting firm that we have encountered.

The Trilogy of Trust

The Trilogy of Trust was our theory that if we could add value to the party to whom we were referred, the referrer's relationship with that party would also be stronger for the introduction.

The critical element was that we needed to add real value, irrespective of whether we were commercially engaged. We needed to respect the referrer's relationship with the party to whom they had referred us above all else, and do nothing to jeopardise that relationship as the bare minimum of our involvement. But the real objective needed to be to add some value, which would leave the business owners favourably disposed to the referrer and the introduction. If we could do this, we believed that our position, as a trusted third party, would strengthen the existing two-way relationship.

Three-way relationships are stronger than two-way relationships and will withstand more challenges and create more opportunities.

So, we went further. We believed the achievement of our objective to add value would engender reciprocity and create a steady stream of referrals from a myriad of contacts and connections.

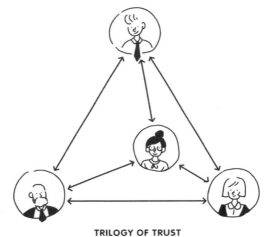

TRILOGY OF TRUST
Reciprocity takes over, over time.

It Works More Quickly in Reverse

What was interesting was that as we gained momentum from the Trilogy of Trust, we discovered it worked far more quickly in reverse, although it was invisible. Most people we know, or are reliably referred to us, are polite and pleasant. On the surface things seem to be going well, so if we make a bad impression we are not going to know straight away. We will only find out some time later, when agreed actions are not followed up, emails are not returned and the referrer who made the introduction for us no longer refers.

Adding Value in Areas that are not Visible

The 9 Paradigms

The 9 Paradigms was the second element that differentiated us. We genuinely respected the vast majority of business owners we met, and did not pretend to be experts in their space. We knew they were *experts* in a few areas, *capable* in a few, and *blind* in a few; and we explained this through the 9 paradigms.

The 9 Paradigms argue that there are generally nine areas of expertise required to take a business to its full potential, and when big enough and successful enough, all businesses employ departments of experts across all nine areas.

THE 9 PARADIGMS
The areas vary from business to business
but are often characterised under these 9 areas.

Not all businesses can afford to employ experts across all nine areas and nor do they need to, as the owner is usually expert in three and competent in three. We did not try to add value in these areas: for one thing, the owners' expertise in three areas was probably greater than ours, and they already had service providers to fall back on for assistance in their three areas of competence. We assumed they already knew what these were, and called for assistance from their service providers when needed. We did not want to be seen as poaching from these service providers who had given us the referral in the first place. So, the other three areas, the areas where they were weak or which they could not even see, was where we needed to concentrate.

However, there was a major problem: because they could not see these weaknesses, they could not see where we could help them. Simply telling them was not going to motivate them.

THE 9 PARADIGMS

It is the areas where businesses are POOR that provide
the greatest potential for others to add VALUE.

Our research showed that the vast majority of accountants and bankers were frustrated by their clients' apparent lack of action when they gave them what they believed was genuine and compelling advice. The reason was simple: while the *issues* were obvious to an objective advisor such as an accountant, the owner only saw the *symptoms*. Usually the accountant had not explained the underlying reasons for the advice, so the business owner was not confident that the advice was necessary – or, indeed, accurate. Somehow, we had to help the business owners see the underlying reasons and impediments for themselves, so they were more likely to act on them, and this required some clever thought!

You do not Need to Reinvent the Wheel

As it turned out, we stumbled across an operation that offered business coaching for private business owners and accounting firms. This operation had developed tools for diagnosing businesses by asking the owners a structured series of questions. The answers allowed them to identify underlying issues facing a business, which could be presented to the owners in a way that made them acutely aware of problems without having to be told outright: they discovered the areas they needed to address for themselves. This felt right for us, based on our assessment of why business owners did not act on sound advice, because it provided a subtle but structured way of highlighting impediments.

We were impressed enough to acquire this intellectual property, and set about tailoring it for use by our organisation. What we learned as we came to understand the process that had been developed led us to join the dots between psychology, perception and the reality of what all business owners go through. This led us to the third element of our unique approach, *The Johari Window.*[1]

---

[1] The Johari Window is a technique created by Joseph Luft and Harrington Ingham in 1955 in the United States

The Johari Window

No One Knows Everything

The **Johari** Window was developed in the 1950s to explain how we can be seeing the same thing as someone else but from a quite different perspective. I came across the **Johari** Window while undertaking my postgraduate marketing qualifications, and believed that the theory could also apply to knowledge.

Put simply, the **Johari** Window is a pattern that shows us how all knowledge falls into four quadrants which allow us to accept as a fact that there are things we know and things we do not know! The four quadrants are referred to as the **OPEN ARENA, FAÇADE, BLIND SPOT** and **UNKNOWN**.

	What I know	What I don't know
What you know	**OPEN ARENA**	**FAÇADE**
What you don't know	**BLIND SPOT**	**UNKNOWN ?**

This resonated with us for a number of reasons.

Firstly, we were not walking into an owner's business pretending we knew everything. We didn't; and we respected the fact that they knew more than us in their core areas of expertise. But there were areas where we had knowledge and they didn't.

More importantly though, we didn't feel compelled to pretend we knew everything.

Secondly, we didn't like conventional consulting approaches that made out the consultants were experts in more areas than they really were, which created a **FAÇADE** of unrealistic expectations as to what they could achieve – often to do no more than to lock in their services and high fees.

Thirdly, we agreed that owners often developed **BLIND SPOTS** about their business, employees, clients and markets – and sometimes about their service providers as well.

How then, could we start to deliver visibility and value?

We needed to engage in that first, and then in all subsequent client meetings. Just as I had learned through my life's business journey, we needed to **ASK** questions that the business owner was willing to answer (i.e. topics they were passionate about), **LISTEN** to their answers (i.e. showing we were genuinely interested), **UNDERSTAND** what was told to us (we had to know the facts) and then, and only then, make suggestions as to the most appropriate next steps.

Our **VALUE** Encounter was born!

CHAPTER 3

Value Encounter Methodology

CHAPTER 3

....

Value Encounter
Methodology

The Birth of the VALUE Encounter

We set about developing a simple framework for use in the coffee or casual first meeting, the first one that opened up the **OPEN ARENA**. It was developed to replicate the structured review process we had developed from the intellectual property we had acquired, and which we could apply as the first step of any prospective commercial engagement. It had to be simple and replicable; just enough structure to reinforce that the meeting was about them, not about us.

We began establishing five critical components to every meeting that we needed to tick off before suggesting any form of commercial engagement. If we could not tick off all five we would not suggest commercial engagement, under any circumstances!

Our five components, if ticked off, ensured we could add value, irrespective of the commercial outcome. It did not matter which order they were ticked off:

1. Visibility

We recognised that not all business owners were prepared to share confidential information with us even if we were reliably referred, so we signed a one-way Confidentiality Deed in their favour as the first formal step in the meeting.

When meeting a prospective client we endeavoured to understand their business, their objectives for that business and the things they saw as priorities. We learned that most private business owners were passionate about their business and enjoyed talking about it. When they explained their business to us, in their own words, they believed that we knew as much as they did. This gave us our first indication of whether we could add value to their business or not, and was based on the need to share: it didn't matter how much pre-meeting research we did or how well informed we were by the referrer – if the owner didn't explain their business objectives to us, we found they assumed we did not know what their objectives were, even if we did. This became our acid test. No sharing of information meant definitely no commercial engagement – we would just pass on a few tips that would reflect favourably on the referrer.

We call this step **VISIBILITY**. If owners do not want to share their business information with us, we can't be sure we can help and we will not try to engage commercially.

We often explained this process as opening up the **OPEN ARENA**!

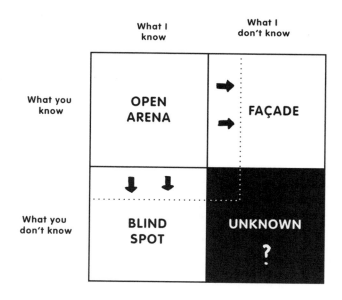

2. Leverage

This was one of the more critical elements to tick off in the coffee meeting.

We figured that if we were genuinely going to add value to a growing business it needed to happen relatively quickly, not in the medium to long term way things moved in the corporate environment we had all worked in until now. Committed business owners want to see results quickly. If they need to buy completely new equipment, install massive new systems or employ entirely new teams of employees they need time, and improvements from our involvement will not occur quickly for them.

We understood the basic dynamics of improving results. It was not about dreaming up a series of strategies and priorities that everyone had to implement. It was about making a number of small incremental and manageable improvements that could be implemented on top of everyone's already hectic schedules.

Two things drive results: activities and resources.

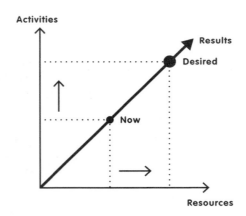

In order to improve any result, we needed to positively change activities or more positively utilise the available resources. We needed to determine whether there was scope to improve the performance of the business by leveraging, or improving the efficiency or effectiveness of what was already in place. If we could not see that this could occur, we knew any improved result or value added was not going to happen quickly enough for the average private business owner.

This is why we always liked to visit a business's premises and walk around the operation. It is also why we needed to talk to the shop floor and to the various levels of staff once we were engaged to undertake a more comprehensive review.

The ability to work smarter, not harder, is what this process is about; and with our major corporate experience we could usually see considerable scope for quick improvements just from a walk and a chat. Even very well-run businesses that offered little in the way of internal leverage provided wider leveraged opportunities such as geographic expansion though distribution, licensing or even franchising. There were a few, however, that had more urgent issues to overcome, such as critical funding, where we were not the right source of assistance. If we could not see a leverageable opportunity it was often prudent to suggest a referral to a trusted party, who could assist them more directly.

3. Understanding

The third area that we needed to tick off was whether or not we could understand the competitive dynamics of the business's markets.

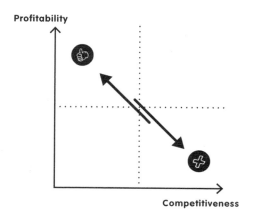

Most businesses want to compete in low-competitive, high-margin areas of their markets – as opposed to high-competitive, low-margin areas. If this is not already the case, they are usually trying to move in that general direction.

If we could not understand the dynamics in the coffee meeting, we needed to be confident before we engaged commercially, that we could understand these dynamics. Our ability to understand and more importantly validate these dynamics, was critical to the effectiveness of our value-added activities. If we could not validate the competitive market environment, our recommendations would be no more than educated guesses, as opposed to validated strategic or operational objectives.

One example of how important this is involved an accounting software company we assisted. The company was on the verge of releasing a new version of their software, which they claimed was light years ahead of their current version. The business had several thousand businesses paying a modest annual maintenance fee and was operating a little better than breakeven. They also had 100-odd dealers who were selling a wide range of software, some of them competitors' products.

Our initial comprehensive review confirmed that they should release the software to all users, insist that they upgrade and then charge substantially more for that upgrade. The charge could be two or three times the current annual fee according to our initial assessment. We also showed how they could organise their dealers to charge all their users for installing the upgrade if it was compulsory. Additionally, a concerted program of training all users in the new areas of functionality would drive considerable consulting revenue.

This was a very courageous recommendation and we would never have supported it if we had not been confident of being able to validate it in the market before implementation. In this case we were confident that we could ask users, gauge the support of dealers and check the quality of the software relative to competitors' products and pricing before making any suggestion of a commercial rollout for the new software.

The company did decide to charge, although not as much as our initial review had indicated and they increased revenue by over 60% with a large proportion falling to the bottom line.

4. Agreement

This was the fourth check. Was there capacity for an agreement between us if there was an opportunity to assist them? We did not mean a protracted, drawn-out exchange of information: we meant agreement there and then. You see, most consultants want their prospects to sign off on concrete agreements, locking their services in for predetermined periods, usually based on exciting (and often unrealistic) expectations of the outcomes they will deliver.

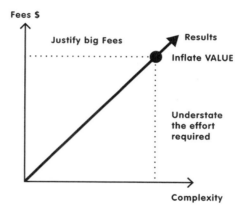

"Conventional consulting approaches"

We knew we needed to share information with each other before we could really add value, and it was pointless embarking on the traditional 'contract me for a year' approach before both parties knew we could add genuine value. If we couldn't help, or more importantly if the owner was not prepared to participate, we risked missing the happy ending, and the Trilogy of Trust would be undermined.

If we breached the referrer's relationship with the business by failing to perform, or by reflecting unfavourably on the referrer, no more referrals would be forthcoming.

If we believed we could help after checking off the first four points, we finished with an agreement on how we should move forward. This was often a high-level comprehensive evaluation tool utilising the review we had acquired and tailored for our use, with the objective of more formally and structurally opening up the **OPEN ARENA**.

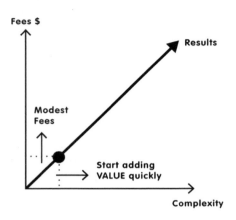

"The **nem** approach"

If we suggested a simple commercial step involving minimal expenditure, a small amount of time and the involvement of their referrer or accountant (if desired) and they baulked, we were not prepared to engage commercially – particularly given our guarantee that if our Comprehensive Review represented no value we would not charge the agreed (nominal) fee. Of course, a formal report would not follow.

What we learned from doing this was that when we moved out of or expanded the **OPEN ARENA** we actually crept together into the previously **UNKNOWN**, learned from each other and identified the priorities that would deliver the quickest possible outcome for the business.

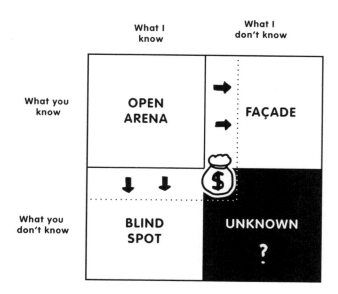

This is precisely what had occurred with the accounting software firm we assisted. The Comprehensive Review enabled us to understand the dynamics of their customer base and market, and it enabled the management to see that charging users for the upgrade was worthy of further consideration.

5. Engagement

This was the fifth check in our coffee meeting and only when it was ticked off did we know we could genuinely add value. We then looked for a verbal commitment to engage us. We found, however, that a small number of owners would sit back and say, 'So how are you, specifically, going to help me and what will you achieve? Give me a proposal together with the cost, and I'll have a look at it.'

We would reiterate our suggestion of some form of an initial high-level comprehensive review at minimal cost, which did not really warrant a full-blown proposal. This would tease out either that there was another decision-maker who needed to be consulted (in which case we would respond with an email outline of our process) or that they wanted to get another quote. In this case we would politely decline to set out a proposal, and state that while we could confirm our process in a brief email we were not able to identify the outcomes or the extent of any value-added outcomes until we had been through the first phase of our review process. What we were really saying was, we are not going to bid blindly for your business.

We would then suggest that they engage with the other party, cautioning them not to sign off on extended work before seeing the recommendations. We would also offer to review those recommendations free of charge in appreciation of the referrer's interest in their business.

You see, these business owners were not **ENGAGED** in our **VALUE** Meeting, were still suspicious and were not prepared to take the first minor step. Our view was that it would be very difficult to add value to a business if the owner was not engaged, so we walked away politely, always offering some free advice or suggestions that would reflect favourably on the referrer.

In this way we developed our **VALUE** Encounter Methodology from our desire to determine if we could add **VALUE**:

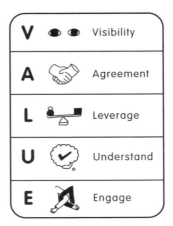

V	👁 👁	Visibility
A	🤝	Agreement
L	⚖	Leverage
U	✔	Understand
E	🧍	Engage

Our approach was unique and successful, and counterintuitive to traditional consulting approaches. While each of us learned to apply the process under different circumstances and with different businesses, it really set us apart from the average consultant.

We were not sitting there telling a prospective client how good we were or how we could help them, because at this stage we often did not know.

Honest Consultants!

Our referrers, after overcoming the initial risks and hurdles of their first referral, were pleasantly surprised by the feedback from their clients. Many saw immediate benefits, through value-added work, direct quality referrals and less fee resistance. Our firm started to become busy. The three of us had more work than we could poke a stick at, and a wide range of referrals.

It was obvious that we needed to expand.

CHAPTER 4

Value Encounter Applied

CHAPTER 4

....

Value Encounter Applied

As we took on new partners we trained them to apply our unique approach we started to observe varying levels of effectiveness with the application of our **VALUE** Encounter Methodology.

While we were all busy we couldn't necessarily guarantee client work to new partners. Our business to date had grown through trusted referrals, and every new partner needed to develop their own pool of referrers to guarantee lead flow. We encouraged them to prepare comprehensive network maps; but despite our coaching and support, we observed some common behavioural traits. One obvious problem was that the people partners often thought would help them the most were helping them the least.

We Go to What and Who we Know

This meant that they gravitated towards people and businesses that they thought matched their desired commercial outcomes –understandable but very ineffective – and once they were having trouble it became very difficult to reestablish contact with the people they had prioritised making contact with, at least quickly. We started to realise from our observations, support and direct assessment of new partners' networks that the level of their relationship with the people whom they knew was critical to the effectiveness of their first meeting.

I knew this from my life's experience in business and moderated my interactions accordingly, but some of my colleagues found it more difficult to gain traction.

What We Do is Not Selling

Another problem was that, despite our **VALUE** Encounter checklist, new partners often tended to dwell on what they did and how they did it instead of finding out more about the other party. As we grew the partnership and became busier, the senior members could not buddy up with new partners in important networking meetings as easily as when we started.

We needed to develop an approach that recognised that our *entire* network was capable of providing valuable connections, leads and commercial opportunities – not just those parts that we *thought* could be helpful.

We also needed to comprehend that when we were drawn into lengthy explanations of *what* and *how* we consulted we appeared to communicate like any other consultant, irrespective of our genuine motivation to engage only if we could add genuine value. We simply looked and behaved as if we were selling!

The success of our **VALUE** Encounter lay in the fact that we were *not* selling. We were learning if we could add value by *listening*.

We acknowledged that sitting in front of a prospective client was different to sitting down with someone in our network. But the network wasn't the end: it was the start of engagement with prospective clients and these prospective clients were just not visible!!! Somehow the **VALUE** Encounter needed to be moulded to consistently unlock the hidden potential of each partner's network of referrers, creating interconnectivity, reciprocity and lead-flow for them.

It Takes Time With Friends

It wasn't until one of our new partners, Joe Maden, came to our weekly meeting complaining about a good friend, a banker, who had bought into a life and risk insurance business, that we joined all the dots.

Joe had failed to engage with the banker, and with many other of his wider network for many reasons. In our weekly meetings Joe continually complained about how his banker (best friend) had never helped him. We suspected the banker was not a real friend! We also suspected that Joe had explained *what* and *how* **nem** operates and had come across as if all he wanted was referrals to the banker's clients. In any event, this came to a head when his best friend was retrenched and ended up buying into a business that specialised in providing life and risk insurance to individuals and businesses. Soon after, he contacted Joe. And guess what he tried to sell him – life insurance. Joe was furious. Rather than dwell on it in the weekly meeting we agreed to catch up later that day.

Put Ourselves in Their Shoes

On investigation it turned out his friend had not really sold to him, but it was obvious that the only reason he had contacted Joe was to sound out his insurance requirements and those of anyone else Joe knew.

His friend was like a mirror – we suggested to Joe that his friend probably felt the same way Joe had when he made contact after contact after contact and got nowhere. Joe would not agree that he had sold in any way whatsoever. I assumed that was the case: after all, I wasn't at the first, second, third or any subsequent meetings. So, I asked Joe if he would put his life and income protection through his friend. The answer was a resounding no!

Why? I asked. Joe gave a whole lot of reasons. They were friends and never really discussed income and other financial matters with each other. He would feel very uncomfortable. If his friend did a bad job, cost more than his existing insurance broker, or couldn't service his needs as well, their friendship would be put at risk. Apparently, the ex-banker really *was* a close friend. Furthermore, his friend had seemed to jump into this new role very quickly, and who knew if it would be a long-term proposition? He was very vague about what sort of equity he held and on what terms, so Joe didn't know if he would stick at it. His friend had never mentioned his insurance expertise in the past and had even expressed dismay in the past at how his bank was enforcing cross-selling into insurance products across their customer base. What if he left his existing service provider only to find his friend had moved on? On and on the reasons went.

Empathy is Not About You

We asked Joe, 'Is it possible that your friend thought the same things about you when you went to first meet him?' The penny finally dropped.

Explaining *what* he does to friends and family could appear like selling, and any sniff of selling could trigger the feelings Joe felt when his friend sounded him out for life cover.

Joe's experience was an important lesson to us all. We set out to redefine the way our new partners networked, within our wider networks and their own.

CHAPTER 5

Value Encounter with Networks

CHAPTER 5

Value Encounter with Networks

We asked new partners to prepare their network maps, either before joining or during the first week or two.

We Are Better Networked Than We Think

When we asked new partners to document their network we noticed that they tended to document only those people they thought were important to them, or would rank them purely on current or potential business activity. Very few even listed their fellow partners! In order to fully leverage our collective wider networks, however, it was critical that they write down everyone they knew, including fellow partners. This was now emphasised, as it was a critical first step to our collective business development activities.

Everyone We Know Can Add Value

A common mistake our new partners made when looking at their broader network was a tendency to identify only individuals who were believed to be important to their new role as a **nem** partner. They were focusing on people they thought could help them or who had perceived relevance to their new role – a perfectly natural phenomenon but a narrow one which we called the iceberg approach: all energy goes towards identifying useful icebergs instead of all the icebergs in our network, seeing only what is on the surface and not what is underneath!

We explained that many unemployed executives have found themselves networking frantically amongst former colleagues, contacts and acquaintances only to find that the people they thought would help them the most help them the least. While some are quick to secure employment and put the embarrassment of networking behind them, many are scarred from the experience and left pondering the values of many of the people around them.

The process we wanted to follow for defining our network was a constant one. When mastered, it had the ability to generate a continuous stream of positive experiences on a professional and personal level because everyone in the network was capable of adding **VALUE** – we just needed to know how and when this was appropriate! We needed to explore what was under the tip of every iceberg.

Understanding Our Entire Network

Unless we are highly organised we probably never fully assess our entire network, let alone document it, and this was certainly the case with our new partners. We stipulated that all networking and business development had to commence with identifying and documenting everyone they knew in a network map.

A network map is best prepared illustratively, on a big piece of paper – butcher's paper is good. Starting with themselves in the middle of a circle, the partners drew circles to include all the different *groups* of people they knew in broad categories, such as:

Clients (if they had existing client activity)
Past clients
Close friends
Acquaintances
Colleagues by company (past & present, including **nem**)
Professional associations
Club memberships
Social associations
Schools (theirs & childrens': tertiary, secondary, primary and preparatory)

The number of groups could be extensive.

The next step was to identify all the individuals they could think of in each of the groups they had identified. This is a fluid process, so we recommended they should expand upon and reassess their groups periodically.

Relationships Can Be Defined

Once this was undertaken we asked partners to characterise every person by the level of the relationship, and *not* according to their perceived relevance or value. We found four criteria, friendships, relationships, contacts and connectors, which were very effective ways of categorisation. These criteria simplified a complex array of the experiences, psychological theories and interactions that we all encounter without necessarily appreciating their significance.

The Relationship Criteria Were Created for Networking

1. FRIENDSHIPS

Individuals that we know professionally, personally or possibly both. From whatever background these people are considered friends. We know a lot about them, have shared many experiences and are confident and relaxed in their presence.

2. RELATIONSHIPS

Relationships refer to those individuals we know professionally or socially, but often not both. While we may know a reasonable amount about them, genuinely like them and enjoy pleasant interchanges, these have not developed into true friendships. There is usually a level of mutual respect with those with whom we have relationships.

3. CONTACTS

Contacts are those people whom we bump into or have been introduced to, but do not really know. They can also be people we have known either professionally or socially at some point, but who are now out of touch. We usually fell out of touch for a reason, and reconnecting can be awkward.

4. CONNECTORS

Connectors are people whose name we know but cannot put a face to, plus everyone else that we do not know. This is everyone else in the big wide world to whom we can be connected: we just do not know how or by whom yet.

1. Friendships

It is interesting that friendships were often relied upon exclusively by our new partners, based on their perception of how helpful their friends could be in the business sector. Our research and life's experiences showed that the people we know the best and look towards with confidence when assessing what we want from our network, rarely assist us directly with commercial opportunities, or in the way that we would hope. Joe's banker friend is a prize example of this. There are a variety of genuine reasons why this is so:

We Are Unproven At Our New Company

While we may carry significant respect because of our past roles and achievements, the position we now find ourselves in may be uncharacteristic (e.g. unemployed) or new to us (e.g. from banker to life insurance salesman). As a result, we carry no proven authority within the organisation or position we find ourselves in, and our opinions may not be taken as seriously as we would like.

Friends May Be Uncertain About Our Capability

Often we may find ourselves in a situation that is new, either in terms of a new direction or new position, and our friends are uncertain of our capability. They are unlikely to refer contacts to us or have confidence until we are proven in our new position. Our relationship may have developed through mutual convenience but this does not necessarily mean the person respects our professional capabilities.

Friends May Not Want To Risk Their Relationship With Us If We Fail

Friends genuinely like us and may not wish to risk our relationship by dealing with us commercially. They would rather keep business separate from the social connection, and are reluctant to assist us until they see we are successful and there is no longer any perceived risk in Engaging Commercially.

They Actually Do Not Like Us As Much As We Think

Often relationships develop from mutual convenience and objectives. We meet each other's partners and friendships develop, common interests bring us closer and it just happens to benefit both of us at a corporate level as well. This does not mean the contact actually likes us as much as we think they do.

We Appear Unprofessional Because We Know Them Too Well

When we connect commercially with friends we are often very comfortable with them. We relax and talk openly; we may not even suit up. As a result, our commercial purpose for meeting does not always match our behaviour, with the result that we come across as unprofessional.

We Approach Our Friends With Too Much Confidence

In addition to a casual approach we may also tackle these meetings with heightened expectations, and as a consequence we are far too confident during our exchange. This can be construed in many ways, but nearly always negatively, especially if we look like we have expectations.

We Start To Sell Our New Employer's Services Or Products

This is like selling Amway products to our best friends. The worst thing we can possibly do with this group of contacts is start to sell. They may accommodate us with an initial purchase because there is no real risk, but they do not reorder, and they will write us off as using them for our own interests.

The Friendship Is Not Based On Mutual Respect

In much the same way as some colleagues failed to help me, and some demonstrated a lack of respect, some friendships are never going to help us, and the quicker we find out, the quicker we can move on! The **FAÇADE** of friendship can continue but that is what it is – a **FAÇADE** – and it is often easier to maintain the **FAÇADE** than disclose the honest painful truth.

Friendships Can Help But We Need To Guide Them

Friends rarely help us straight away with a direct commercial outcome; it can occur but it is very rare. Knowing this, **nem**'s objective was to involve friends indirectly, by introducing us to someone or somewhere that could help us. Alternatively, they could reconnect us to someone that we had lost touch with.

It was important that our new partners were conscious of their entire network when meeting friends. Refreshing their past common networks to identify **CONTACTS** that the friends were still in touch with who could be reintroduced to the partner. When reintroduced the right way (i.e. their friend introduces the contact personally which allows the partner to refer to the meeting) these **CONTACTS** can be elevated to a **RELATIONSHIP** status.

The theme of all our new partners' meetings with friends, after initial pleasantries, was to introduce their new role and quietly explain the opportunity and what they saw ahead for themselves at **nem**. They needed to be relaxed (as they should be with friends): to be themselves and answer questions instinctively. They should not try to score points by answering questions as if there was a service or product solution that they had access to.

We emphasised that partners should never canvass for direct commercial outcomes with friends, but should know them well enough to ask for assistance. If the friends ranked their friendship at the same level as the partner, they would genuinely want to assist if they could. This is a bit like knowing a good friend has a particular issue that they find seemingly insurmountable. We naturally want to help, and if there is no prospect of being able to help directly we try to think whom we can refer them to, or how we can connect them with who may be able to assist. In fact, if we can't think of anyone we are disappointed and sometimes quite upset.

FRIENDSHIPS are therefore wonderful referrers to connect us to people we do not know. Their introduction, if undertaken effectively and conscientiously, may bring those **CONNECTORS** to **RELATIONSHIP** status very quickly. For example, if we are business consultants, as our new partners were, one valuable source of referral is accounting firms. Accounting firms are very difficult to engage with, as they have to fend off a plethora of snake oil salespeople trying to make contact with them and gain access to their client base – so they adopt a wide range of techniques to avoid engaging with people who try to make contact. **FRIENDS**, however, could refer our new partners to accountants they knew, or even to their own personal accountant. With a personal request from them to their accountant, that accountant becomes a **RELATIONSHIP**, promoted from **CONNECTOR** status.

The Next Step Always Needs Positioning, to Not Jeopardise Friendships

While this may appear straightforward, new partners still needed to go into meetings with some outcomes in mind. Irrespective of how the conversation moved they needed to be comfortable enough to say, 'Look Fred I would never expect you to engage me commercially but it would be really beneficial to me at the moment if you could introduce me to any accountants, business bankers or lawyers that you know.' If they say they don't know too many, a reply could be, 'Just one would be fine, even if it is your personal accounting firm.' This is when we find out their view of us and their willingness to assist. Those who genuinely care will in fact set up an introduction or start to think of people that could help us; those who do not, we have misjudged.

So friendships are wonderful sources of referral. The key is to develop approaches that do not jeopardise the friendship but leverage their network for our benefit. The cleverer our strategy (that is, the more steps it moves us away from them) and the less it looks like selling, the more effective these referrals will be. And friends and family are also wonderful for practicing the **VALUE** Meeting process; experiencing the power of listening and understanding and accepting brief, articulate explanations of what you do.

When we are networking for new business opportunities (as our new partners were), the need to develop open, broadminded strategies cannot be underestimated. It may not be referrals to accountants – we may not even have a source in mind – but it is critical to plant the seeds of how friends can help, and the more removed they are from the direct commercial outcome, the more comfortable they will be.

You Do Not Know Where Friends Will Take You

An example of how narrowly we think, particularly when we are anxious for results, comes from one of our new partners, Michael Harvey. Michael worked at BHP and accepted a redundancy a year before joining **nem**. He dabbled in private equity and consulted a little before joining. When he joined he completed his network map and graded his network according to our guidelines.

Despite the development of a wide range of sound relationships – his own, our partners' networks and **nem**'s wider network – Michael failed to gain commercial traction quickly. Like many new partners, we believed, he had failed to grade his relationships accurately. It is a common problem for new partners to overstate the status of their relationships, and a tendency to believe their network has a higher appreciation of them than they actually do.

Eventually we agreed to a catch-up, and Michael sat down with his network map. As we explored his gradings and questioned their accuracy, he started to break down. He was under unrealistic expectations from his wife, and was feeling the burden of a very young family. He had been charging very low fees. Now he was at his wit's end.

I took my pen, closed my eyes, and dropped it onto his network map.

I hit a Friendship. It was the CEO of a major subsidiary of BHP. I had him!

We Are Not Always Right

'So, Michael, you have this guy as a Friendship... surely he is a relationship?' (My corporate experience told me that it might be a relationship not based on mutual respect).

Michael perked up, showing quite a bit of anger and courage. 'I see him every week at least. Our children go to the same school and I even catch up with him socially for a beer at the local pub. Sure I met him at work but our lives are inextricably linked and we really are good friends.'

I was taken aback by this, and puzzled, I asked why he had not yet met him over coffee during working hours, as opposed to social activities. His response was typical of the networking patterns of partners that were established before we understood relationships. 'He's a CEO. He doesn't know any small to medium business owners and I certainly wouldn't want to compromise him by asking for contract work at BHP!' he exclaimed.

Friends Can Give Us Access Not Business

I said, 'Sure, but could you have a coffee with him at the drop of a hat?' 'Yes,' he replied. 'And would he take the conversation seriously?' 'Yes,' he said. 'And do you think he would genuinely like to help you?' 'Yes,' he said. 'So if during the coffee meeting you said, "Look I don't want you to compromise you in any way but knowing how **nem** operates would you mind referring me to the head of procurement?" what do you think he would say?'

'He would do that as long as he was comfortable with the reasons,' Mark said.

'So you are now in front of the head of procurement on the strength of the CEO's referral,' I said. 'Do you think the head of procurement is going to take you seriously?'

'Of course.'

'So you now explain how **nem** operates and ask the head of procurement if there are any small to medium suppliers of products or services that they value but are creating issues for them relative to consistency in service or quality: would he take that question seriously?'

'He might,' said Michael.

'And now you are in front of the business owner referred by possibly their largest customer, do you think they are going to take your introduction seriously?'

'Yes' Michael replied.

That strategy played out, and Michael was off and moving very soon after this, and never looked back.

2. Relationships

These people are not known well enough for us to hold many preconceived views of their capability or their wider networks. There is usually mutual respect between both parties and meetings tend to be professional even if they are not business related.

These people are the engine room of commercial referrals. There are a few reasons for this:

- They don't know us well enough to consider the relationship to be at risk from business.
- They understand we are there for business, even if we know them only socially, and they are not afraid to refer to their network provided they see a need within it that we can help with.
- Like us, they can build credibility from helping their network.
- They are often referred to us from a friendship, making the association even stronger from a professional standpoint.

Nearly all of us would prefer to rely on a referral from a reliable source than go through the time-consuming exercise of looking for solutions ourselves. The trick is to know which parts of our network are genuine, reliable reference points. They are the **RELATIONSHIP** group!

Bias Exists In Some Relationships

To illustrate the point, my mother was eighty-five years of age when Dad passed away suddenly at age eighty-seven, and she was determined to stay in the family home, living independently. I live nearby, as do the rest of the family. We were all determined to assist Mum to maintain her independence in her own home for as long as she could. My experiences working at the geriatric home when I was young had made me very determined for this to occur, and I was not swayed by the glossy brochures my sisters produced from time to time.

As she lives by herself, frozen meals are organised for a few days every week. We all visit quite regularly and do a bit of cooking for her, and occasionally as a treat she is taken out to a local restaurant by my older sister.

One Saturday when I popped over she was having lunch (another frozen meal), and she said to me she had had a wonderful evening during the week at a new local Chinese restaurant. She went on to explain how the food was simply superb and she recommended that I should go there!!

Knowing my mother's taste (she likes frozen meals!) and her enjoyment of going out, I immediately removed the restaurant from my list of venues.

My mother is a **FRIENDSHIP**, I have preconceived views of her habits, tastes and behaviour, and I cannot take her endorsement as reflecting my own tastes.

So home I went to do the lawns and a little gardening, when my neighbour came over the road to say hello and we chatted about business and what we had been doing on a relatively superficial, friendly level. I like my neighbour - he is a similar age and owns his own business, and our kids mix a bit together. Then he said, 'We had dinner at that new Chinese restaurant last night with the kids. It was really very, very good. You should give it a try.' This is a **RELATIONSHIP**, and because I have respect for him and do not know him too well, I took that referral seriously and now started to reconsider the new restaurant.

As I returned to the gardening a fellow I know from around the corner, but whose name I was unsure of, was walking past. He overheard my neighbour and added, 'You should try that new Chinese restaurant, it's really great.'

If this had actually happened (it didn't), the referral would appear insincere. It would mean very little – in fact it would seem strange, as if he had an interest in the restaurant. This is the quality of a referral from a **CONTACT**. Neither of us knows the other well enough to have anything to risk from the referral.

Effective Engagement – We Filter Out, Not In

Differentiating between **RELATIONSHIPS** and **FRIENDSHIPS** is critical to effective engagement. Engagement does not necessarily mean commercial engagement. It can be as simple as having people listening to us and understanding what we are saying. This may sound basic, but we live in a world that is saturated with information and varying forms of communication. In order to cope we scan information and deal with most communication superficially. We are brutal in determining what we will absorb, and filter out more than we filter in.

So if our partners sounded like they were selling, or sounded like traditional consultants, the people they were communicating with would filter them out very quickly and pigeonhole them into the consultant's box and that would be it. Dead end.

This is a subject in itself and a few of our partners specialise in the **NEW SELLING** phenomenon that is sweeping our society. We no longer want to be sold to. We can research most products or services ourselves. Let's take a new car. The internet has transformed our ability to assess the different models to the point where we have made up our mind to purchase before we see the sales representative. If we are going to buy a particular car we do not want a traditional features-and-benefits pitch – we want our assessment (and quite possibly our decision) reinforced. We want confirmation of the benefits to us, and the price.

A 'now generation' salesperson will ask open exploring questions and understand our needs before positioning the car to reinforce them. They will undertake a **VALUE** Encounter to determine if they can add value (i.e. that the product or service meets our needs and pricing requirements). In some situations, they will help us to confirm that the product does not absolutely meet those needs, and will suggest an alternative product, service or path.

3. Contacts

Contacts are people we know but are now out of touch with – and if we are out of touch there is usually a reason! They can also be acquaintances or people we have bumped into that we know superficially, or have not known for very long. As a consequence, those people are the most difficult to make connections with.

A common approach by our new partners was to try to reconnect with contacts they thought could be useful to them. This approach is like cold calling. It is awkward and often insincere (and viewed as such by the contact); and even if a meeting is organised the outcomes are usually far from helpful.

Even if the partners actually liked meeting these people they usually only gravitated towards those whom they thought could be useful to them. They deliberately reconnected, often quite forthrightly, so even if they caught up, the coffee meeting was often viewed with suspicion by the contact.

Many new partners started to attend events to network with people they did not know, often through associations or common interest groups. While there was nothing wrong with this, there needed to be an understanding that the commercial prospects were very limited. In fact, in the ten-odd years we have been running **nem**, not one partner has ever obtained a commercial engagement as a direct result of meeting someone they did not know at networking events. Some work has come from such events, but only when a partner has reconnected with a **CONTACT** and re-established a past **RELATIONSHIP** without overtly making contact with them.

Contacts have nothing at risk from referrals or from taking up our time.

Contacts Never Give Us Business

A common networking outcome is when a new partner meets someone at a networking event for the first time. That person is now a contact. The contact asks the partner if he has expertise in a specific area, to which he replies yes. The contact mentions an opportunity to pitch or tender or put in a proposal to do some work. The new partner is very accommodating, calls on the resources of the firm and enthusiastically prepares a proposal after appropriate research. He may even prepare a tender.

The closer the partner gets to decision time the more excited he becomes, often believing there is a 50/50 chance of winning the business and ignoring the advice of the firm. Our advice is that there is no real prospect of engagement – and guess what? No new partner has ever won work from blindly networking and pitching to **CONTACTS**.

Our advice is not to pitch unless we are absolutely sure we can establish a **RELATIONSHIP** status (mutual respect) within the time it takes to make the brief and pitch. This is rarely achieved except by reference back to **FRIENDSHIPS** or **RELATIONSHIPS** that can favourably influence the decision makers of the **CONTACT** *without* appearing to circumvent the probity of the process. Our partners would be better off saying, 'The firm does have the expertise required, but unless we can understand the real underlying needs, can develop the appropriate business relationship and are confident in adding real **VALUE** we are not prepared to put forward a proposal.'

We Can Always Say No!

Contacts can generate business, particularly if we have endorsed a product or service, or are reliably referred, but a relationship based on mutual respect must be developed or inferred by the referrer. This can occur far more quickly when we refuse to pitch or tender. It can occur even more quickly for low risk, low value products or services; but without a referral or reconnection from a **FRIENDSHIP** or **RELATIONSHIP** it can take time for more complex product or service offerings. When this is the case both parties usually lose interest in each other if business does not occur quickly, and the contact remains just that – a contact!

Finding common connections through our **FRIENDSHIPS** and **RELATIONSHIPS** can often be very helpful. The development of an introductory touch and staggered contact approach may also be considered (e.g. Christmas cards, newsletters, LinkedIn connections, introductory letters, etc.) prior to making contact. The reality, however, is that referrals from **CONTACTS** are not as reliable as **FRIENDSHIP** and **RELATIONSHIP** referrals, so we recommend that new partners do not solicit contact before they have exhausted **FRIENDSHIP** and **RELATIONSHIP** lists.

4. Connectors

CONNECTORS are everyone that we do not know… yet!

We call them connectors because they can enter our network through a variety of avenues, as we will explore later on.

As we often say when we make common connections through people we do not know, 'It's a small world'. In fact, one study of this phenomenon became known as the Six Degrees of Separation: anyone we wish to make contact with is only six connectors away from us. While the technology platforms of today and our increasingly sophisticated social networks may provide a quicker avenue, the original work has been shown to still hold true.[1] That is: any person we wish to contact is only six people (connectors) removed from us.

Direct networking amongst **CONNECTORS** is very difficult but surprisingly very common. The unsophisticated networker sees opportunity where there is no inherent **RELATIONSHIP**. Some people can keep knocking on doors to have them slammed in their face. While the persistence and drive required to cold-call can be useful qualities, the approach is largely ineffective unless we have a strategy like looking for common connections, we are disciplined in our approach, and we actually enjoy the process of introducing ourselves to strangers.

Most **CONNECTORS** of any real value will come to us through a referral from a **FRIENDSHIP** or **RELATIONSHIP** or a **CONTACT,** resulting in contact or a coffee meeting that has mutual respect through association, upgrading the unknown **CONNECTOR** into a **RELATIONSHIP**.

The Coffee Meeting Process!

With this knowledge and understanding of their relationships new partners were encouraged to undertake varying **VALUE** Encounter Meetings with their network and to follow the process developed for this specific purpose. We called these meetings 'Coffee Meetings'.

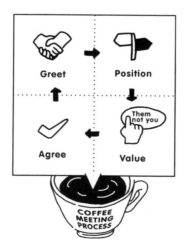

---

[1] Internet experiments have found that there are still six degrees of separation using email. See Duncan Watts' work, *Six Degrees: the science of a connected age*, Norton, 2004

While each meeting would have varying emphases depending on the relationship (who introduced whom and a variety of preconceived objectives) the process required the partner to turn the coffee meeting around to learning more about the person who they were meeting rather than to explain what **nem** does.

Even with friends who were genuinely interested, after a brief explanation of why they joined **nem** the partners were encouraged to turn the meeting back to finding out more from them about their objectives and in doing so, finding avenues to add value to them.

Those partners joining **nem** who took the time to understand their relationships, graded them according to the criteria **nem** had established and followed the coffee meeting process started to gain commercial traction much quicker than those who didn't.

The **VALUE** Encounter approach (of not selling) still required considerable effort, but we started to see demonstrable improvements in activity, referrals and lead flow.

A few partners also started to apply the approach with clients who wanted to grow and needed new client activity. Those were often professional service providers that were starting out, or businesses that could not rely on their existing clients or networks, or businesses that required up-and-comers to bring new business without canvassing existing clients.

Tradespeople, graphic artists, accountants, lawyers, financial advisors, risk insurers, bankers – to name just a few – who were introduced to networking redefined quickly generated referrals and developed lead flow through more effortless engagement.

Works More Quickly with Existing Clients

It was not until a four-partner accounting firm asked **nem** if the same approach could apply to client networks that **we** realised the breadth of the application of the **VALUE** Encounter Methodology.

The accounting firm had embraced our networking relationship criteria, and redefined and trained its senior up-and-coming staff to network for new business with marked success. But the firm also wanted to develop business from their existing clients. Like many accountants, they just didn't like to engage with their clients overtly because it felt like they were selling.

Chasing New Business Ahead of Existing Business

Up to this period, **nem** had relied on relationships with business bankers for referrals and had many levels of embedded relationships that generated continual lead flow. As we grew, however, it became increasingly difficult to expand the number of banking relationships in proportion to the firm's growth. It just took too long to build relationships with business bankers, as their focus was almost entirely on new business. If the new **nem** partners could not provide immediate leads for the business bankers they were introduced to, the relationship would not develop; but as it took time for new partners to develop a network that would produce positive lead flow, it was impossible to meet the bankers' expectations.

What was occurring was a culture of chasing new business at the expense of developing the relationships they already had! This phenomenon had spread to all the banks.

One aspect of business bankers' activities, which puzzled **nem** and stood in the way of developing relationships quickly, was the emphasis on finding new customers. They were so busy chasing new clients they did not know that they had no time to build relationships with **nem** (unless we provided endless referrals) or to understand the potential of their existing client portfolios.

The accounting firm's request and **nem**'s knowledge of the business-banking sector enabled our redefined networking criteria to be extended to existing client portfolios. It was then that we developed **ELEPHANTS, TIGERS, CATS** and **KITTENS** as categories for existing client relationships.

CHAPTER 6

Value Encounters with Clients

Just as our partners used to look at their networks to find out who was capable of helping them the most with direct commercial outcomes, we found businesses doing the same thing with their clients.

Clients are almost exclusively categorised by some real or perceived monetary value for the service or product provider. Once graded, the service or product providers interface with their customers according to their perception of that value.

We at **nem** had all been brought up in business applying a similar approach, and there is nothing inherently wrong with it. A number of techniques of varying complexity have been developed over the years to help businesses identify the future stars and how to milk the cows. But at the end of the day all conventional approaches are focused on which customers are the most important, or could be most important. The what's in it for ME (WIIFM) factor. This is perfectly understandable, but we found it very ineffective and inefficient, particularly with embedded client portfolios and relationships, where we tend to focus on what we *know* and what we can see.

Treating your customers as **ANIMALS** is new. It challenges conventional approaches and will unlock the hidden potential of the relationships that you hold and transform the way you do business!

All conventional approaches fail to address the iceberg theory: that what we see on the surface is only part of the picture. To see the entire picture we need to look deeper.

The level of relationship that we have with each client is critical to seeing more of the picture. The lower the level, the poorer the visibility; the higher the level of relationship the more visibility; but often, too much visibility or familiarisation creates **BLIND SPOTS** and biases, which we will touch on later.

Once the level of relationship is known, a strategy for each encounter with each level of relationship can be developed and applied to accelerate the business development potential of that encounter. So the **ELEPHANTS, TIGERS, CATS** and **KITTENS** categories were developed for much the same reasons that we developed **FRIENDSHIPS, RELATIONSHIPS, CONTACTS** and **CONNECTORS** for our wider networking.

Which Animal is Our Customer?

As a general rule the following applies to each category.

1. Elephants

Elephants were chosen to represent friendships, as they live for a long time and have long memories. Those who that fall into this category have been customers for a long period of time, so you both know a lot about each other. If they are not large customers, they have usually followed the path of their customer or client service manager's career within the organisation.

It is easy to feel very comfortable around Elephant customers, although we know they can do a lot of damage if they get angry or decide to leave. The fact is they can squash us without knowing it. They usually know a lot of other Elephants. We try not to upset our Elephants; and if they leave it has a bad impact on our business. On the other hand, Elephants are capable of great largesse.

As with friendships, *bias* creeps into Elephant relationships, and both parties can start to take elements of the relationship for granted.

2. Tigers

Unlike Elephants, clients who are Tigers cannot be taken for granted. These clients mean business, so we are always on our guard. There is always that nagging competitive threat and we know they are prepared to move if we are unreasonable, or will commit to other suppliers or service providers if they have to.

Like us they are efficient, and ready to respond to any negatives or positives. There is usually a degree of price or fee sensitivity, so there is always justification of value on the agenda.

Tigers keep us on our toes, and because of this there is underlying respect, usually for one another's needs for mutually beneficial outcomes.

3. Cats

Cats are clients with whom we usually have a good working relationship, but they are not as active as Tigers. As a consequence, we usually only have some of their business, and we are not on our guard as much. These clients, like Kittens, can be relied upon to remind us when they want something – in fact, they can be relied upon to pester us to get what they want if they have to, a tactic deployed by them to obtain priority over our Elephants and Tigers.

Where client portfolios are concerned, most service or product providers have more Cat clients than Tigers or Elephants.

When Cat clients become large enough and we move to handling all their business, they can move silently into the Tiger category. To achieve this transition usually takes a great deal of time and effort, which many product or service providers do not have, because they are busy attending to their Elephants and Tiger relationships.

4. Kittens

These clients are usually small, like Kittens. They are not taken too seriously and, in some client or customer portfolios, we do not even know their names.

We really only have shallow or impersonal relationships with these clients primarily because there are lots of them. Because of their numbers they can get in the way of more important business opportunities and really be a nuisance. Some businesses cull their Kittens every so often for this reason.

While this is usually based on hard commercial analysis, the reality is that businesses are getting rid of customers and clients with whom they have a very low relationship and about whom they have a very low level of knowledge. **nem** argues that we do this at our peril.

Every Kitten is capable of growing up to become a Cat– we just have to give it a name and nurture it. It doesn't have to be the senior or most experienced person doing this; it can be done by trainees or graduates. In much the same way as children look after a Kitten when we bring it home, young enthusiastic employees will relish the opportunity of nurturing and interacting with small customers or clients. And only when Kittens are brought into the home, given a name, fed and looked after will they grow into cats.

If we do this with our small clients, they will grow into cats! And every Kitten has parents (i.e. more Cats) and is related to many other Kittens.

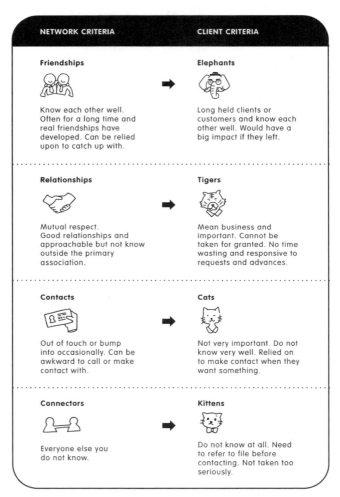

VALUE ENCOUNTER ®⃝ CRITERIA

NETWORK CRITERIA	CLIENT CRITERIA
Friendships	**Elephants**
Know each other well. Often for a long time and real friendships have developed. Can be relied upon to catch up with.	Long held clients or customers and know each other well. Would have a big impact if they left.
Relationships	**Tigers**
Mutual respect. Good relationships and approachable but not know outside the primary association.	Mean business and important. Cannot be taken for granted. No time wasting and responsive to requests and advances.
Contacts	**Cats**
Out of touch or bump into occasionally. Can be awkward to call or make contact with.	Not very important. Do not know very well. Relied on to make contact when they want something.
Connectors	**Kittens**
Everyone else you do not know.	Do not know at all. Need to refer to file before contacting. Not taken too seriously.

In broad terms these categories of clients align with our wider networks and carry many of the same **RELATIONSHIPS** attributes. The difference is that clients are established as a result of business, so our relationship with them develops based on that business or perceived level of future business. What **nem** has discovered, however, is that the same relationship levels develop across client and customer portfolios as across our wider networks.

When the four-partner Accounting firm asked **nem** if they could use the **VALUE** Encounter relationship to develop business from their existing clients without sounding like they were selling something, the first thing we asked the accounting practice to do was to show us their existing grading criteria. This looked like the most traditional network grading or client grading criteria as follows.

TRADITIONAL GRADING CRITERIA

NETWORK CRITERIA		CLIENT CRITERIA
People that you believe will help you directly with your business outcomes and have connection or relevance to your desired commercial outcome. A network priority.	(A's)	Big important clients/ customers that you cannot lose OR have significant perceived potential for growth. You spend a lot of time with them and they are a priority for events.
People that may be able to help you directly with your desired commercial outcome but you are not entirely sure. Secondary priority.	(B's)	Important clients but not capable of being A's. Can afford to win and lose a few. Secondary out bound priority. Backups for events and functions.
People you are out of touch with or people you know through associations that may be able to assist you but you need to reconnect. Low Priority.	(C's)	Smaller clients/customers with limited business and not seen as a priority at all. Contact is minimal and impersonal.
People that you believe cannot help with your desired commercial outcome. Do not bother contacting.	(D's)	Insignificant customers/ clients that you do not know at all. Contacts left to impersonal mediums and periodic requirements.

Then we asked them to overlay the **VALUE** Encounter relationship grading across their existing client base.

When we asked the firm to overlay the **VALUE** Encounter relationship criteria of Elephants, Tigers, Cats and Kittens on the dynamics of the portfolio, it changed significantly. Interestingly, all subsequent applications have tended to reinforce the dynamics, which we found in the first client application.

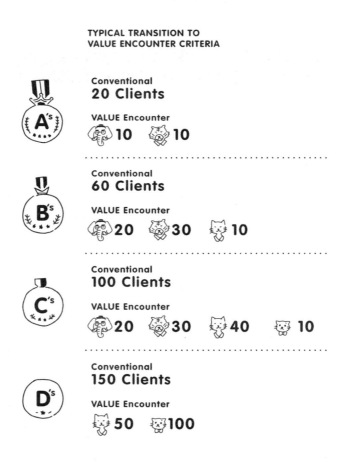

**TYPICAL TRANSITION TO
VALUE ENCOUNTER CRITERIA**

A's

Conventional
20 Clients

VALUE Encounter
10   10

B's

Conventional
60 Clients

VALUE Encounter
20   30   10

C's

Conventional
100 Clients

VALUE Encounter
20   30   40   10

D's

Conventional
150 Clients

VALUE Encounter
50   100

A grade clients: Only one-third to a half of those clients are actually Elephants. Just because they are large and important clients that you spend a lot of time with, does not mean they are close enough to be regarded as Elephants. Many are often Tigers, who you cannot take for granted and never feel totally comfortable around.

B grade clients: These comprise a combination of Elephant, Tiger and Cat relationships. Usually due to the length of time they have been clients and whom they have dealt with over that time.

C grade clients: Similar to B grade clients but due to their smaller monetary value some also fall under Kitten relationships.

D grade clients: These usually only come under Cat and Kitten relationships. Due to their size they rarely develop above Cat relationship status although there are usually a few odd exceptions.

Relationship Basis

The same biases that exist within our networks exist within our client portfolios.

The closer we get to customers, the more we know and the more both parties take each other for granted. This is a two-way process, as we found when we scientifically tested our approach within the banking sector.

Once the level of relationship is accurately identified, a contact strategy for each level of client relationship can be developed to counteract this bias and accelerate the commercial effectiveness of the relationship.

The contact strategies developed under the **VALUE** Encounter Methodology can vary widely between industries and within individual businesses, but remarkably, these strategies have been found to be extremely effective across a wide range of businesses that **nem** has assisted.

CHAPTER 7

alue Encounter Tested

CHAPTER 7

Value Encounter Tested

In 2008 a partner in the firm, agreed to test our **VALUE** Encounter Methodology in the business-banking sector.

This was a sector well known to our firm. From our inception we had developed a close working relationship with one of Australia's leading business banks. On the strength of multiple levels of relationships, the firm referred a lot of deals to the business bankers we knew, and vice versa. As we grew, however, the bankers focused almost exclusively on new to bank business (i.e. new clients) as opposed to getting to know all their clients (i.e. Elephants through to Kittens) better. It became far more difficult for us to obtain referrals from business bankers.

This was exacerbated by the global financial crisis, and is even worse today as all banks have reduced client-facing staff and increased client portfolios.

What Customers Really Want

The first stage of the research confirmed what we saw in many organisations: those who undertook research tended to focus on issues and measures that were important to them. The results, no matter how well or independently conducted the research, were biased.

As business bankers and their clients were the participants in the research, we will look at banks' traditional research initiatives.
Say you are a business bank client and rely on the bank for financial support and an array of financial services and products. You will have varying levels of interaction with the bank, and varying views as to its service levels. Your dependence on it will create varying views, opinions and biases.

For example, your bank may be imposing onerous conditions on your loans by asking for rapid repayment of principal, increasing interest rates or charging excessive fees for commitment breaches. You are angry, but know there is nothing you can do in the current business climate. You need its loans and can't afford to switch banks. When an independent researcher rings you and asks a series of qualitative and quantitative questions regarding the service you receive and your satisfaction levels, what do you do? You probably grade the bank satisfactory out of fear of damaging your unsatisfactory but essential relationship – of upsetting the apple cart.

On the other hand, your business may be bulletproof. The banks have to be kept honest with rates and margins and you often play a couple of banks off against each other to get the best deal. In this case, your response to the same survey questions might be quite different – you would have no difficulty or hesitation in adversely grading the banker.

These are responses that evolve from the levels of dependence, service and relationship experiences that we have. The banks use their research as benchmarks from period to period, so the results show trends. But they are inherently biased.

To eliminate these biases, the research asked business owners what they considered the most important service and product criteria provided by their business bankers. They were then asked to grade their business bankers' delivery against those criteria. Business bankers were then asked to self-assess their performance against the same criteria. The research was independent; as it was not commissioned by the banks. It guaranteed the anonymity of all participants.

The following is a summary of the top five criteria identified by business banking customers, their satisfaction with their business bankers' delivery against those criteria, and the business bankers' self-assessment against the same criteria.

Total Group

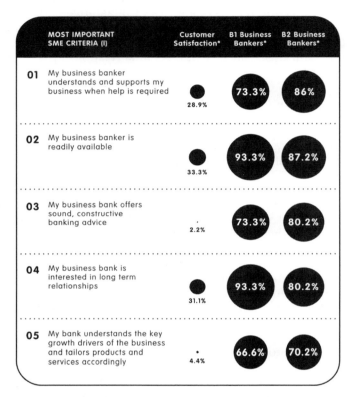

MOST IMPORTANT SME CRITERIA (i)	Customer Satisfaction*	B1 Business Bankers*	B2 Business Bankers*
01 My business banker understands and supports my business when help is required	28.9%	73.3%	86%
02 My business banker is readily available	33.3%	93.3%	87.2%
03 My business bank offers sound, constructive banking advice	2.2%	73.3%	80.2%
04 My business bank is interested in long term relationships	31.1%	93.3%	80.2%
05 My bank understands the key growth drivers of the business and tailors products and services accordingly	4.4%	66.6%	70.2%

(i) Extract from Dr. Ian Freeman's Doctoral Paper: Seeking Synergy in SME Financing. An examination of the dichotomy existing between the needs of banks and small-to-medium business enterprises (SME's) in the Australian business banking context.

* Percentage of customers and business bankers that agreed or strongly agreed with their banks' delivery against the SME criteria.

You can see 29% of customers rated their banks as meeting or exceeding their expectations for their most important service criteria – the two business banks' bankers rated themselves as 73% and 86%! This was not, and is not, a bank bashing exercise! It is typical of what we have found in many businesses.

Every business that conducts outbound research has by its very nature created bias. Nearly all research questions are developed around what the business believes is important in relation to the quality of its products and services. Questions in relation to what clients find important are usually presented as voluntary questions and subsets of existing themes.

A bias that routinely occurs is for account managers, business development managers and sales representatives to overstate their clients' satisfaction with their firm's products and services. In fact, the more businesses know about their clients, the wider the satisfaction gap becomes. This is due to **RELATIONSHIP BIAS,** and addressing this is the cornerstone to more effective business development. Eliminate or counteract **RELATIONSHIP BIAS** and the business development results are infinitely more effective.

Eliminating the Bias – THE INCUBATOR!

Having independently and anonymously identified business banking clients' satisfaction levels against the same criteria with their business bankers and their business banks' view of their service levels, it was time to test the **VALUE** Encounter Methodology. One of the two banks that participated in the research commissioned the firm to test the **VALUE** Encounter in one of their business banking centres (BBC). The one chosen had been one of the bank's worst performing BBC's for some years.

The *first step* involved preparing a Client Services Grid. This grid expanded on the typical financial criteria to include all other products and services on offer, with a tick under each indicating whether or not the customer utilised these particular products and services.

Typically, businesses already have a list that grades clients according to some level of actual financial performance or potential financial performance. In this case it was annual gross margin contribution. Ranking was in order of value – no other criterion. This bank also had an automated report that showed the products each client utilised, or did not utilise, which was effectively a Client Services Grid – easy so far!

The *second step* was to create a Relationship Matrix for the bankers that would accurately define the relationship that they had with their customers. This involved interviewing each business banker (there were eighteen) and their client-facing support staff; that is, the office support staff who interacted with clients on routine matters or on behalf of the business banker.

The following are the Relationship Criteria established for the bankers.

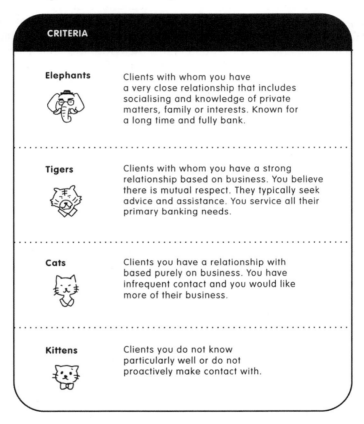

CRITERIA	
Elephants	Clients with whom you have a very close relationship that includes socialising and knowledge of private matters, family or interests. Known for a long time and fully bank.
Tigers	Clients with whom you have a strong relationship based on business. You believe there is mutual respect. They typically seek advice and assistance. You service all their primary banking needs.
Cats	Clients you have a relationship with based purely on business. You have infrequent contact and you would like more of their business.
Kittens	Clients you do not know particularly well or do not proactively make contact with.

The *third step* was to ask the business bankers to grade each client according to the Relationship Matrix Criteria developed in step one. While this is relatively straightforward, some individuals found it difficult, as they had not routinely thought of their customers in this way. It is important, however, that a concerted effort is made to grade customers correctly and consistently.

The *fourth step* was to introduce the **VALUE** Relationship measurement tool, which needed to be completed for each of the Elephants, and where possible applied to Tigers. This process for Elephants is required because a colleague, preferably the boss, needs to be briefed prior to a meeting, to validate the answers or fill in the knowledge gaps in a **VALUE** Meeting with an Elephant client.

This **VALUE** Relationship measurement tool consists of up to twenty-five questions that are prepared for the specific business that is applying the **VALUE** Encounter Methodology.

All questions are linked to the following key themes:

Vision	The owners' vision for their business – what is it?
Aspirations	What do they want to do when the vision is achieved?
Leverage	Have they referred business to you and you to them?
UCA	What is their Unique Competitive Advantage?
Empathy	Do you like them – do they like you, honestly?

Elephant VALUE Meetings

There are many reasons why a primary relationship manager needs to measure the Elephant relationships and *not* run the **VALUE** Meeting:

1. They usually have known the customers for a long time, so more than likely the customers believe they know everything about their business. If knowledge gaps are apparent to the clients (when asked by the relationship manager), then this may not look very professional and could make them reassess the sincerity of the relationship. It is perfectly acceptable for a colleague or the boss, who does not have regular contact, to ask such questions.

2. These customers are usually of long standing, and bringing in a more senior colleague is seen as a sign of importance and respect. The clients appreciate the gesture.

3. The colleague or boss can usually offer referrals, connections and wider opportunities with their network than the primary relationship manager can. This creates reciprocity and creates

an environment where the client is more open to helping the bank.

4. The next commercial steps can be suggested by the colleague or the boss, without any negative reflection on the primary relationship manager, so the risk of raising the commercial next step is mitigated.

5. By introducing the boss or senior colleague their relationship is elevated to one of mutual respect through the primary relationship manager's Elephant relationship – and business can flow.

The *fifth step* was to expose each participant (bank managers and office staff with direct client contact) to the **VALUE** Meeting.

The **VALUE** Meeting is a non-sales encounter. While the **VALUE** Meeting we developed as consultants was designed to determine if our firm could add **VALUE**, the **VALUE** Meeting for embedded or existing clients was much simpler. It just needed to start the clients talking so they would share information – without feeling they were being interrogated.

There were always the meet and greet pleasantries etc., but when the time was right the meeting needed to transition into a question about the clients' business. The structure consisted of five critical elements:

1. Vision   What is the clients' vision for their business or personal affairs?

When we say vision we do not mean to ask them what their vision is, instead ask questions about what they want to achieve from their business.

2. Ask: Open questions. If we are asking about the business or their personal objectives, we cannot help asking open questions. They are easy and unthreatening – and guess what? – clients love talking about their business.

3. Listen: Listening: not interjecting. Let the clients talk, listen to them sincerely and absorb what they are saying. It's that simple. Too many professional training programs and client interview formats consist of checklists and questions that need to be asked. The

VALUE Meeting just wants us to listen – no insincere interjection to pitch our next question!

4. Understand: Understanding: what is being said to us. If we do not understand, we should note it, and at an appropriate time (and this is the only time we should interject), ask. This is particularly important if there are technical acronyms, or aspects of the discussion, where we don't understand what is being said. We get very few chances to ask genuine question like this. If we do not understand, and we do not ask there and then, or at an appropriate time in the VALUE Meeting, the clients will assume we know. Worse still, we will feel embarrassed to ask later, which can be particularly trying for less experienced staff.

5. Empathy: Empathising: this must be shown and genuine. By showing we care we are conveying a sincere understanding of what they wish to achieve.

This is the **VALUE** Meeting!

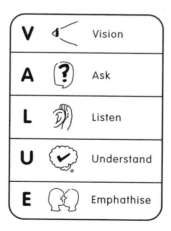

V		Vision
A		Ask
L		Listen
U		Understand
E		Emphathise

And it really is that simple, no matter how demanding the clients are.

This step did not require role-play, in-depth training or communication techniques – just an understanding of how to position the meeting, and the need to vary this according to the level of the **RELATIONSHIP**.

The *sixth step* was to understand how to make a **VALUE** Call, which was straightforward. It was the same as the **VALUE** Meeting but undertaken over the telephone by the office staff.

A **VALUE** Call was to be applied exclusively to **KITTENS** with whom the relationship was very low; it usually took two **VALUE** Calls a reasonable period apart, with reference to the notes from the first **VALUE** Call, before a **VALUE** Meeting was worth being organised with the banker.

With these **SIX STEPS** the bankers and their support staff were asked to grade their clients according to the **RELATIONSHIP** Matrix developed for them, and to conduct varying **VALUE** Encounters based on those relationships.

ELEPHANTS: Measure the **RELATIONSHIP**. Brief a colleague or the boss to run the **VALUE** Meeting and have them filling the knowledge gaps or confirming the answers.

TIGERS: Undertake a **VALUE** Meeting. If the client is particularly demanding, it could be advisable to measure the relationship first and buddy up – but this was each banker's call.

CATS: Undertake a **VALUE** Meeting.

KITTENS; Support staff or the banker undertakes at least two **VALUE** Calls as a lead up to a possible **VALUE** Meeting.

Meeting the Animals

Off they went! And over the next ten weeks, with only minimal intervention, the BBC conducted 476 **VALUE** Meetings and made 397

VALUE Calls, reaching 37% of their clients.

To the delight of the bankers, over the twelve weeks of the program (two of preparation and ten of **VALUE** Encounters) they were not required to undergo any other forms of training, conduct any of the routine telemarketing cold calls, or work with any of the various industry specialists that routinely expected the bankers to create sales opportunities amongst their clients for insurance products (life, risk, etc.), brokering, leasing, foreign exchange, financial planning products, etc., etc.

After the ten weeks of **VALUE** Encounters the clients were asked to reassess the performance of their business bankers against the same service criteria.

These were the results:

MOST IMPORTANT SME CRITERIA (I)	B1 Customer Satisfaction	
	Before Incubator	After Incubator
01 My business banker understands and supports my business when help is required	13.3%	90.6%
02 My business banker is readily available	15.6%	92.0%
03 My business bank offers sound, constructive banking advice	2.2%	85.4%
04 My business bank is interested in long term relationships	11.1%	90.6%
05 My bank understands the key growth drivers of the business and tailors products and services accordingly	2.2%	86.6%

(i) Extract from Dr. Ian Freeman's Doctoral Paper: Seeking Synergy in SME Financing. An examination of the dichotomy existing between the needs of banks and small-to-medium business enterprises (SME's) in the Australian business banking context.

How Did the Animals Respond?

The results were simply staggering, and consistent with the experience of **nem** when applying the **VALUE** Encounter Methodology in other businesses. The simple process of conducting a **VALUE** Encounter changed the customers' satisfaction with their service providers significantly, to levels that other international research in the business banking sector indicated was the tipping point for client advocacy[1] – that is, the level at which clients willingly refer their bankers to other businesses and people that they know.

What's In It For Me?

In the harsh commercial world, the old adage 'show me the money' was still the key measure, and this too showed a remarkable result. Throughout the ten weeks of the **VALUE** Encounter pilot each banker was required to record each **VALUE** Encounter and each commercial opportunity, if any, that was clearly identified during the encounter. This could not include extensions to existing business, like increasing an overdraft or rolling over existing facilities. It could also not include vague opportunities, or opportunities that arose outside these meetings, for instance if a customer rang them or the office. They could only record identified, quantifiable commercial opportunities that occurred during their **VALUE** Meetings or **VALUE** Calls.

At the end of the ten weeks the bankers had identified the following commercial values:

---

[1] Extract from Ian Freeman, 'Seeking synergy in SME financing: an examination of the dichotomy existing between the needs of banks and small-medium business enterprises (SMEs) in the Australian business-banking context', unpublished PhD dissertation, Southern Cross University, 2011

Chapter 7: Value Encounter Tested

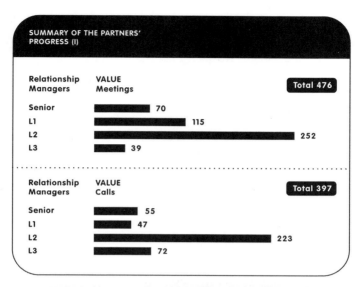

SUMMARY OF THE PARTNERS' PROGRESS (I)

Relationship Managers	VALUE Meetings	Total 476
Senior		70
L1		115
L2		252
L3		39

Relationship Managers	VALUE Calls	Total 397
Senior		55
L1		47
L2		223
L3		72

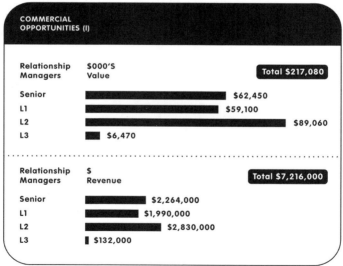

COMMERCIAL OPPORTUNITIES (I)

Relationship Managers	$000'S Value	Total $217,080
Senior		$62,450
L1		$59,100
L2		$89,060
L3		$6,470

Relationship Managers	$ Revenue	Total $7,216,000
Senior		$2,264,000
L1		$1,990,000
L2		$2,830,000
L3		$132,000

(i) Extract from Dr. Ian Freeman's Doctoral Paper: Seeking Synergy in SME Financing. An examination of the dichotomy existing between the needs of banks and small-to-medium business enterprises (SME's) in the Australian business banking context.

This bank's key measure was margin, and the $7.2 million in new opportunities represented a staggering 34% of the BBC's annual budget. Unfortunately, the research did not extend to tracking the conversion of these opportunities, but the BBC's performance improved significantly over the following four months. It went from one of the worst performing BBCs to one of the stars, and has continued to maintain that status at the time this book was published, some two years later.

The results of this research correlated to a wide variety of wider industry applications undertaken by **nem**. Despite this, the bank in question never embraced the **VALUE** Encounter more widely.

> *Little old nem did not have the Fortune 500 status to intervene with the bank's training initiatives, not that it is traditional sales training (they didn't understand that either!)*

Be assured, that one day the **VALUE** Encounter Methodology will be taken seriously by the banking sector, and those banks that grasp the methodology first will gain an unprecedented competitive advantage.

CHAPTER 8

Value Encounter Experiences

CHAPTER 8

Value Encounter Experiences

What we have learned?

While some experiences can be put down as exceptions and not the rule, there are a number of factors that routinely occur as a result of the successful and consistent application of **VALUE** Encounters with Elephants, Tigers, Cats and Kittens.

First, the formula is simple common sense. This causes some seasoned and successful professionals to claim the approach is what they do anyway. Understandable, but when applied to their Elephants in the way we advocate, opportunities, knowledge and connections almost always emerge which expose their **BLIND SPOTS** and lack of client knowledge. In addition, these same seasoned professionals can rarely explain why their approach works, and certainly cannot train less experienced staff.

Second, less experienced staff or lower level staff like Julie who will be referred to later (The Plodder) rarely deal with (or lead client relationships with) highly sophisticated clients, who are generally handled by more experienced staff. We have found that the **VALUE** Encounter approach is extremely well received by the clients of lower level and less experienced staff.

Third, the **VALUE** Encounter quickly identifies clients' needs and opportunities for value-added products and services, in addition to generating reliable referrals.

These are delivered without the service or product provider having to sell (in transactional, cognitive or strategic selling terms), effectively eliminating the most awkward aspect of traditional sales techniques. This makes the **VALUE** Encounter Methodology particularly powerful for industries such as Accounting, Banking and Finance, or those where the business development people do not come out of traditional sales and marketing disciplines.

Fourth, irrespective of whether or not there is an immediately obvious commercial opportunity or outcome, the client's attitude towards the service or product provider changes immediately as a result of the **VALUE** Encounter, and this change is almost always favourable, increasing satisfaction to levels that have been proven to turn clients into advocates: that is, to the point where they are happy to refer. This change also reduces pricing sensitivity significantly.

These benefits only occur if those who undertake the **VALUE** Encounter do what they say they are going to do, follow up conscientiously, and keep the rest of their organisation (which may now interact as a result of the **VALUE** Encounter) informed and make sure they also do what has been agreed to.

We call this *table* manners!

Table Manners

This may seem a strange name for such an important process, but it is really very appropriate. When **nem** was starting to grow rapidly, we were showing an increasingly large number of partners the **VALUE** Encounter Methodology and monitoring their progress. Those who were not gaining traction (lead flow) in their networks and ours displayed a tendency not to follow up appropriately and keep the referrer informed. Some (very few) also did not do what they said they would do; and those who did not keep everyone in the communication loop appeared (at least to the clients) not to be doing what they said they would do at the conclusion of their **VALUE** Encounter.

As I was struggling with this and trying to understand how this could occur I was conscious of the increasing demands of the firm on my family time. I was now working long hours, as I had in the corporate world, leaving before my boys went to school (Ben was ten and Seann five) and getting home only in the last minutes before bedtime.

I made a point to clear my diary for a whole week so I could take the boys to school each morning and be home in time for dinner at night. That meant getting into the office no earlier than 9 am and leaving by 4.30 pm.

So the week started...

I dropped the boys at school by car with no conversation and no real appreciation on Monday – the reality being that they slept in as long as they could, which made it almost impossible to walk or ride their bikes although the school was quite close. That night I was home by 5 pm and greeted the boys with great affection, only to be ignored. Even my wife seemed annoyed that I was home, as I got in the way of her routine. When dinner was ready for the boys, mine wasn't. I got my meal at the usual time.

Not that it was the same as the boys'. They had an arrangement like a restaurant menu they could select from. Then they ate in front of the television in the back room. They barked orders at their mother, argued with each other and ate like little heifers. I was quite disillusioned. Having told my wife of my objective for the week, I had expected a family meal. Silly me: the house operated like I wasn't there.

I continued without saying anything, and Tuesday was not much different. I was becoming disillusioned and disheartened.

On Wednesday I cracked. The boys were arguing with each other all the way to school (thankfully not a long journey!), and when they got out of the car, Benjamin, the older boy, said to his brother, 'Bye Seanny, have a good day.' Benjamin is a caring sensitive boy, and despite the argument in the car meant what he said.

Seanny replied, 'Bye arse-nugget.'

I cracked. I worked late that night to catch up on work and was seriously questioning the values of our household. How could they behave like that? How could they avoid their dad, or at least not care? It bothered me for the rest of the week. It wasn't until the weekend, on a visit to my parents, that the penny dropped.

Grandma and Grandpa

My parents were in their early eighties at the time and lived nearby, in the family home I grew up in. We dropped in most weekends, but every month on a Sunday Mum would cook a roast. Dad insisted on a proper sit-down meal in the dining room, so that is what it was.

My sister and brother-in-law were coming on this particular Sunday. As we were trying to get Seanny and Benjamin in the car we were met with angry disapproval. While they both loved Grandma and Grandpa, Seanny in particular hated the Sunday roast. It meant he had to eat properly and sit at the table. Normally you wouldn't want to be between him and a McDonald's chicken nugget – a junk food fiend at five. He carried on so badly it was embarrassing, but eventually we got to Grandma's and his tantrums subsided as he started to play with his cousin.

When the roast was ready the kids were rounded up and strategically placed around the dining room table so as not to annoy each other and cause chaos. They sat there like little angels. I almost fell off my chair when Seanny said, 'Grandpa, can you pass the salt please?' He even ate, albeit very, very slowly, some of the roast beef and vegetables. Benjamin was eating civilly and holding his cutlery correctly, and Jessica their cousin was equally well behaved.

I observed in disbelief. Our children knew the table manners we had brought them up with; they just chose not to observe them at home, where they felt they could behave as they wanted without significant and immediate consequences.

It became apparent that day that my children were no different from our firm's partners and many business development people I had dealt with. We all start to disregard or forget our table manners once we are familiar with our environment, whether it be home, our networks or work.

In fact, the closer we get and the more comfortable we are, the worse our manners get. In the case of family, it is even more complicated as emotions freely interfere with logic.

So now we had the analogy, and a name for doing what we said we were going to do, holding colleagues accountable and keeping everyone informed… Table Manners!

1. Elephant Developer

A seventy-two-year-old Chinese immigrant had arrived in Australia with nothing forty-five years ago. He had worked extremely hard, and invested in property on a modest scale before undertaking his own construction projects. He had amassed a property portfolio worth a conservative $70 million and had a debt facility of approximately $20 million.

He did not bank at the BBC where the research was carried out, but the manager of the BBC undertaking the research, Michael, was also responsible for another BBC, and the developer banked there. So, Michael asked if he could run a **VALUE** Meeting with this Elephant client, just to assess its effectiveness, as no Elephant client meetings had yet occurred under the pilot. We agreed of course, although the results could not be included in the incubator program.

With that agreed, Michael asked Roger, the business banker, to answer the 25 **VALUE** Encounter Relationship questions. Roger had banked the client for seven years, the last three as the Lead Manager. He believed he was very close to the client. He knew the client's wife quite well, knew many of their personal affairs, and had met their three children several times.

Without going through all the questions in detail, these were the business bank's understanding of the 25 **VALUE** Encounter Relationship questions.

Vision:	The client was winding down development activity and was expected to retire in the next two to three years. This was evident by the gradual reduction in borrowings, which was once as high as $40 million against $60 million of property and projects.
Aspirations:	Roger was vague about the client's aspirations, suggesting only that he would retire and pass the property portfolio to his children and expected grandchildren.
Leverage:	There were no notable referrals to or from the client. Roger had sold life policies and key man insurance

when the client was in his mid-sixties, but the policies were not renewed after he turned seventy. There were no notable referrals to or from the client as Roger did not want to get in the way of the very profitable core business activities.

UCA: Roger could not identify the client's unique competitive advantage other than to explain that he had developed a close network of predominately Chinese construction contractors and architects, designers and property specialists. The net worth of the client had come from developing multi-unit and apartment complexes of moderate size (of ten to twenty units) and only selling those needed to repay the cost of the development.

Empathy: Roger really liked the client and believed the client liked him as well. They never had any issues. Pricing was never challenged, but Roger had always ensured the client received very competitive rates and fees as the facility had always been secured by the property and guarantees of both husband and wife.

With this briefing, Roger organised a meeting with both husband and wife over lunch with his manager Michael. When they arrived Roger exchanged the usual pleasantries before he introduced the reason for bringing out his manager. It went something like the following:

Roger (business banker):
Thank you for taking the time to meet with us. As discussed, my manager, Michael, was keen to meet you. You're an important client to the bank and Michael wanted to meet and understand your business from your perspective, rather than just reading the file.

Michael (manager):
Thank you, Roger – and that is all we're here for, to enable me to meet both of you and to better understand your business. You've built an impressive business that appears to be slowing from a construction perspective.

What are your plans for your business over the next few years?

AND THAT WAS AS SIMPLE AS IT CAN BE.

Client: Well, I'm winding down slowly, and not prepared to keep developing properties.

Client's wife: He would if he could, but we're expecting our first grandchild soon – so no more long days. Seventy-two is too old to keep working just for the sake of it. We have more money than we need.

At this point Michael, based on the briefing he was given, tried to validate Roger's understanding of the clients' vision.

Michael: I understand from Roger's notes that you intend to pass the property portfolio onto your children at some point?

WITH THIS THE SEEMINGLY MILD-MANNERED CLIENT BECAME UPSET AND RESPONDED QUICKLY.

Client: If I have said it once I have said it a hundred times: my children will get nothing.

Client's wife: They got their education and were given their first homes when they got married and they are all doing very well, so they do not need our money.

Michael: I'm sorry the notes on the file are obviously not very accurate, but $50 million odd is a lot of property, so what are your plans for the properties in the future?

AND THE CLIENT OPENED UP.

Client: I arrived in this country with nothing, illegally by boat seeking asylum forty-five years ago. I risked my life and the lives of my relatives at home if it was ever known what I had done. They pretended that I went to the city to look for work, never to be heard of again.

I came from a rural province that today remains underdeveloped. In fact, it is only in the last nine or ten years that I could return without fear for my safety and the wellbeing of my family at home in China. We have travelled back and forth extensively ever since, and what I would really like to do is to help the children growing up there get access to an education like my children had, without having to risk their lives like I did to do so.

Michael: So you are thinking of a charitable fund or vehicle then?

Client: Yes; but my contacts are limited and I don't know whom to trust to ensure there is longevity and proper process.

Michael: Our network of philanthropic families and vehicles is really very extensive, so I'll make some enquires and see if we can connect you with the right people for advice and assistance – if that is all right with you?

Client: Of course it is, and it would be greatly appreciated, as I would like the income to be channelled to China, not the assets.

Michael: Yes of course. I'm sure you will achieve a great deal with the income but with the greatest respect, the income from the properties will not be a lot of money given that your plan is very ambitious, so you may need to consider benefactor status of an existing institution and not necessarily controlling the structure.

Client's wife: Well, I have some money also. When Dad died his business was passed to the children and I sold my interest to my brother and sister.

Roger: But you were never in business?

Wife:	No I wasn't, but my dad was and my brother and sister worked in it. I brought up our children then did charity work, and never had a real interest in the business. So when Dad died my brother and sister, who chose to stay working in the business and run it today, they paid me out my share.
Roger:	Really! How much did you sell your interest for?
Wife:	The advisors to the entire family handled the transaction so I'm not really sure what the value was but I ended up with $170 million on deposit.

AND GUESS WHAT? It was not on deposit with this bank!!!

In disbelief Michael and Roger returned to the office after a very pleasant lunch – over which they were too embarrassed to raise the bank's desire to hold the $170 million and assist with financial advice. This was intuitively the right thing to do, even if it was for the wrong reason: to overtly sell to the opportunity that is revealed in a **VALUE** Encounter would have relegated the meeting to a sales call.

The correct approach was to agree to a next step, which would deal with the opportunities without suggesting solutions. In this case Michael agreed to consult internally to find some good contacts in the philanthropic world in China, and Roger agreed to get someone to help him to explore the best way of holding the funds owned by the wife! When they got back to the office Michael accessed the files, which went back twenty-three years and nowhere was it noted that the wife was the daughter of the owner of a major well-known retail chain.

Twenty-three years!

> *This is a dramatic example of the biases and BLIND SPOTS that develop over time. The bank did not know she was the daughter of the owner of a major retailer and the clients did not know the bank could help them with the holding of the funds. The bank had only ever lent them money and had never shown interest in deposits.*

The bank did end up holding the funds, and were also directly referred to two other developers of similar size who were unhappy with their own banks. This resulted in considerable new business.

These numbers were excluded from the official incubator pilot as they did not bank at the BBC where the pilot was being undertaken. *But the children did!*

2. Kittens – Children of an Elephant

One of the pilot BBC's Kitten clients was contacted by telephone by a business banker's associate, who undertook a **VALUE** Call (the same as a **VALUE** Meeting but over the phone). During this **VALUE** Encounter the client revealed his ambition to dabble in small local developments. As a consequence of this insight the associate noted on file a prospect of the client borrowing more funds in the future. He currently borrowed $2.5 million against conservative current valuations of $5 million. The rental yields did not quite cover interest, but he earned over $1 million a year gross income as a medical specialist.

The associate put a high priority on the file and a reminder to re-contact them in week ten of the pilot program. The second **VALUE** Call did not repeat the questions undertaken ten weeks earlier. After pleasantries and reacquainting, the first question during the second **VALUE** Call was, 'So what do you want your property portfolio to look like ten or twenty years from now?'

The client explained that since he was a small child he had been around building sites with his dad so he wanted to try his hand at development and to build a property portfolio of considerable value. With a better start than his father had, he expected to create a portfolio value of at least $100 million before he retired from active medical activity.

The associate was staggered by the response and asked what his father did. The client explained a little bit about how his dad had emigrated with nothing and had amassed a small fortune in property.

The associate asked if a meeting could be scheduled with their business banker at a convenient time to discuss business in more detail and face-to-face. The client was delighted.

The two **VALUE** Calls recorded no commercial outcome in the BBC where the pilot was being undertaken. Just two **VALUE** Calls recorded as statistics. But the subsequent **VALUE** Meeting did uncover the fact that the Kitten was the son of the Elephant property developer who banked at another BBC. So the pilot, in the opinion of our firm, would have led to the same outcome that had occurred at the other BBC.

The three children of the developer were in fact, all categorised as Kittens at the BBC undertaking the **VALUE** Encounter pilot. Each of them had modest borrowings in the range of $1 to $3 million, principally as a result of negatively geared property and share portfolios.

The children were 'D' clients before being classified as Kittens. They did not have a relationship with their bankers and no one knew who their father was at the commencement of the **VALUE** Encounter pilot.

It's a small world.

Let's recap how many companies treat their Kittens: too small to worry about; too many to service properly; when they want something they are annoying because there are more important clients.

Kittens are Connected

In animal talk, every Kitten has a precious life. Every Kitten knows lots of other Kittens. Most Kittens grow up to be Cats and are related to and associate with many other Cats.

Selling a Kitten off is like trying to drown it. We do harm to our relationship with that Kitten, and to a multitude of others we do not know about. To ignore Kittens means to ignore their potential to grow with us, and their ability to connect us to their communities is never known and that potential is never realised.

We are not saying that if we look after every Kitten we will earn great connections or outcomes, but ignoring them will ensure we don't.

The best strategies for Kittens are to find ways to have **VALUE** Encounters that are efficient and effective. Not just periodic sales calls. Use them to train non-client-savvy staff or new staff, or even find ways of making inefficient Kittens pay more or walk away of their own account. One client once argued that this is just business and selling them off does little harm. True, it is just business and often understood as such – but if the relationship ends so does any prospect of connecting with their **UNKNOWN** community.

3. The Plodder

Another consistent outcome from applying the **VALUE** Encounter Methodology was also observed in the pilot program during the evaluation phase, when every business banker, non-client-facing support staff and industry specialist (financial planner, foreign exchange expert, leasing expert, etc.) was interviewed to understand their roles, their interactions with clients and their definition of their relationships. As a result of this process each person's experience, expectations and views became known.

One person who really struck us during the pilot was Julie. Julie was in her early fifties and had been with the bank for twenty-eight years. She had undertaken postgraduate studies but had only mid-ranking or middle level seniority. Business bankers half her age were routinely operating in a higher graded role with nowhere near her level of experience. Julie was asked why this was the case, and she gave the following explanation:

'I joined the bank as a mature age teller and studied for my degree part-time. I just completed my studies when I fell pregnant, and I went on to have two more children, working part-time for five or six years. When I returned to full-time I secured a business-banking role in the same branch and I've been here ever since.

'I'm not ambitious and have passed up many promotions because I want to stay at this branch. We had a big mortgage, and my husband's sudden death resulted in only a modest life insurance payment, meaning I really struggled for five or six years to keep my head above water while raising the children. With only a small family network it fell on me to support the children in every respect.

'I do not consider myself to be a technology-strong banker, but I do know just about everything there is to know at a procedural level. Probably because I don't run around blowing my own trumpet and do not appear ambitious I am often overlooked. I earn the least of any banker at my level, but I bear no grudge at my age. I am really happy doing what I do. I know my clients well and I enjoy helping the continual stream of younger bankers and their support staff to navigate their way around the bank's cumbersome systems, approval processes and protocols. With my children now quite independent, I am looking forward to winding down over the next few years and hopefully of retiring when I am fifty-five.'

During the ten weeks of **VALUE** Meetings and **VALUE** Calls, the progress of each previous week's encounters was assessed as part of the BBC's normal weekly sales meeting (8 am on a Monday morning – go figure!). The protocol established was for the three senior managers, or team leaders, to meet with the firm first and get their feedback about the previous week's activities. On the completion of that process, which took about fifteen minutes, their teams would be asked to join together and their team leader boards were compared.

The team leader boards recorded the number of **VALUE** Calls and **VALUE** Meetings undertaken by each team member, plus the value of possible new business that emerged specifically as a result of those **VALUE** Encounters. For some reason activities were not recorded under individual names, just under their levels or grading. This meant we could not see individual performances. During the fourth Monday meeting one of the senior managers, who was not a particularly nice person, started to criticise his team for its overall poor performance relative to the other two teams.

He singled out Julie as a plodder and someone with limited technical product knowledge, only working standard hours and seeming to lack the drive to have a real go at undertaking **VALUE** Meetings. This young, ambitious and clever banker showed contempt for Julie, and seemed to be positioning her as the primary reason for his team's lagging performance.

Not a lot more was said before the teams joined the meeting and they were asked to put forward their experiences over the past week. The team leader boards were tabled and the teams asked to come forward with any questions or learning from the previous week's activities.

The usually quiet Julie started:

'I can't believe how straightforward a **VALUE** Meeting is. I've been with the bank for twenty-eight years and undergone every course ever offered – that is, technical product courses and sales training courses. None of them have ever been that helpful. In fact, I really am very weak on technical product areas that fall outside core business banking activities. I also dislike having to sell, and have never been able to develop productive selling skills as they have been taught.

'But the **VALUE** Meetings are so easy. All we need to do is exchange the usual pleasantries, then ask the owner how the business is going and where they would like to see it in a few years' time. Once the client is talking I just sit back and listen for opportunities to help them grow and achieve what they want to from their businesses.

'I had twelve **VALUE** Meetings last week, taking my total to fifty-one, and have identified over $40 million in new transaction values from these meetings, which can be followed up. I am hopeless with financial planning products and services, but the **VALUE** Meeting makes it very clear if the client needs them! When this is the case I merely close the meeting with the next step of introducing the right person for a subsequent complimentary, no-obligation chat.'

Her senior manager sat silent when the financial planning product specialist interjected. 'Julie your numbers are even better than that, because the clients you introduced me to, Frank and Wendy who run the motel, have also introduced me to his parents and I'm talking to them today. They inherited $15 million last month and are at a complete loss about how to manage their fortune as they were totally unaware of their brother-in-law's fortune when he died.'

Julie asked when his meeting with the parents was, and the financial planning specialist said next week. Julie responded positively, pointing out that they would appear on the next team leader board if the client's referral was accurate.

Needless to say, the senior manager sat silent as we tracked Julie's progress over the ten-week period. Not only did she have real confidence around business development, but she was generating high referral levels and was the single most successful banker in the program. The Plodder was the winner, and a vocal advocate of the **VALUE** Encounter program.

4. An Elephant Pilot

That same senior business banker took nine weeks to organise his first **VALUE** Meeting with an Elephant client. Needless to say, he thought the entire **VALUE** Encounter process was obvious common sense, and something he did in the normal course of his business. He finally selected his largest client, a property developer specialising in industrial estates: extremely profitable, well secured and a significant borrower.

The client was in his late sixties, and the senior banker's answers to the **VALUE** Relationship questions went something like this.

Vision:	Winding down to retirement but not until seventy or even seventy-five.
Aspirations:	Not really known.
Leverage:	None he could think of. Too profitable a client to risk selling Mickey Mouse products unnecessarily or life insurance to.
UCA:	Industry knowledge, zoning expertise and the ability to acquire property before zoning changes occur.
Empathy:	Yes, good friends really. Lots of corporate entertaining with other halves as well. They liked each other a lot.

Armed with the answers an appointment was made with his boss Michael, the same manager who had uncovered the unknown client deposit of $170 million a few weeks earlier.

They met at the client's office and exchanged the usual pleasantries, with Michael being appropriately introduced by the banker. Michael explained to the client that he just wanted to catch up and understand his ambitions for the business and where he saw things going over the next few years. With that open question, the client started to explain.

'I love this business. I started it forty-odd years ago when I obtained rezoning approval for three adjoining residential properties to multi use.'

Michael asked, 'From residential to business use? That's unusual – why did you do that?'

'Yes, you're right, it is unusual. Many developers are preoccupied with rezoning to residential because the density is allowed to be higher and the returns better. But in this case the three houses, which I inherited from my uncle, were very close to a retail area, and were rundown and in need of significant amount of renovation in order to attract reasonable rent. The commercial retail rental area of the precinct was in demand and the rents quite high; retail tenants held longer leases and were required to make good – all positives relative to residential options. So I did my homework and had the area successfully rezoned to accommodate four shops and five two-storey residences above them.

'I was fortunate that my uncle had three adjoining properties, as I was able to overcome most of the covenants that prevented smaller properties from achieving the same rezoning. I cleaned up with that development by selling the residences and keeping the shops. Then I concentrated on acquiring land that was capable of moving to industrial use. It was cheap and less costly to develop than residential, and tenancies were usually long term.'

Michael said, 'You've built up a significant industrial development business by just about any standard and have extensive holdings of land and tenanted industrial properties. Where do you intend to take the business over the next few years?'

He replied, 'I just love the business, and will keep working in it until I drop.'

Michael asked, 'So – any aspirations beyond the business that will see it move to family as you get older?'

The owner became quite abrupt. 'I have no direct family. Married twice with no children, and I was the only child in my family, in fact the only child of my father, his brother and his sister. That is why I inherited the three properties forty years ago. Eventually I want the staff and current manager to own the business, but I intend to work in it until I drop! I'll start reducing hours in the coming years, as I love my rural property and will eventually commute.'

'Isn't the rural property in Bowral?'

'Yes.'

'That's three hours away and a huge commute.'

'Yes I know.'

'So, how many days will you work then?'

'Every day if I can!'

Michael was about to express his dismay when the owner added, 'My helicopter does the trip door to door in 30 minutes. Come on and I'll show you – do you want to fly over the estates and land I hold in the area?' He led them to an area of the estate where the helicopter sat.

The business banker was embarrassed as it was clear he did not know his client flew a helicopter to work.

They went for a forty-five-minute joy ride and as a result of the meeting Michael made a number of connections with other business owners who also flew and financed helicopters.

Some of these were targeted potential clients of Michael's and he obtained some valuable referrals and direct introductions as a consequence of the **VALUE** Encounter.

5. Freight Company's Tigers

Well before **nem** ventured into the banking sector with Ian's doctoral research, an accounting firm in an industrial area of Melbourne was seeing many clients' revenue falling dramatically. This was having an enormous effect on cash flow and a blowout in their own receivables. As this was just after the start of the global financial crisis they were deeply concerned, as many businesses were. They did not really want to know about the **VALUE** Encounter or how they could improve their lead flow, client satisfaction levels and clients' fee resistance, but they were paralysed by the poor trading state of a large number of their clients and the impact on their cash flow.

Understanding this, **nem** partner Bill Ball offered to help an accounting firm's client on a pro bono basis: that is, for nothing. The proviso was that the client had to be in trouble, wanted to participate in a small program, and *had to* commit to at least trialling our recommendations.

With that clearly understood, one of the partners in the accounting firm identified a long-held client in the transport industry who historically turned over about $9 million per annum, was modestly profitable and had been a client of the firm for over fifteen years. While the business never generated a huge cash surplus, the second-generation family owners used the business as security, and for funding a progressively larger and larger property portfolio.

Over the previous six months, turnover had fallen to little more than $7 million. While the business was still modestly profitable, thanks to the assistance of the accounting firm in recommending and persistently driving cost reductions and fleet consolidation, their bank had them on watch as they now fell outside the lending covenants for their properties and specifically for interest coverage.

The offer by **nem** was greeted enthusiastically by the owners, and with a need to act and no fees being paid to **nem**, no one wasted any time. The **nem** partner's objective was to deliver the biggest gain quickly.

Their Relationship DNA

The first and most critical stage of any **VALUE** Encounter program, no matter how similar the business is to others where the approach has already been applied, is the evaluation stage. This stage requires every client-facing and client-support staff member, and their management, to be interviewed, to assess their relationship with their customers. This evaluation process enables a highly relevant, customised and internally sensitive Client Relationship Criteria Matrix to be prepared that relates specifically to the business.

This is the business's Relationship DNA. Not taking the time to discover the Relationship DNA demotes the **VALUE** Encounter process to the same level as any other systematic training process.

The **VALUE** Encounter Methodology is *personal*. It is the business's language, their staff's language, their acronyms and abbreviations, and just as importantly their client-facing staff's creation! They all feel they have contributed to it because they have. They all get a say and can relate to their Relationship DNA.

It took three solid days at the freight company's premises to interview over thirty individuals before the company's unique Client Relationship Criteria Matrix could be developed, validated and put into their matrix.

The following was a guide to the categories established for this company:

Elephants: Long-established clients that the owners knew personally. Half were large customers, but there were quite a few smaller ones as well. No real pricing or service pressures. Considered long-term loyal customers.

Tigers: Customers where the company had all their business. Not known personally to the owner, but the sales team knew basic interests, such as the football team they followed. Not friends, but a healthy respect. Usually price and service delivery sensitive, and kept the company on their toes.

Cats: Similar to Tigers, but the company knew they did not have all their business.

Kittens: Small insignificant customers with infrequent amounts of activity. No meaningful contact. They phoned the freight company when they wanted something.

With time pressures it was decided to concentrate on Tigers. When the business looked at their traditional grading of existing customers as As, Bs, Cs and Ds there were a lot of crossovers, as expected. The company wanted to concentrate on Elephants for referrals and Cats for new business, and they argued vehemently for this approach. But Bill held his ground, quoted the agreed mandate and insisted that the **nem** approach at least be trialled.

With that reluctantly agreed, the logic was explained:

1. Elephants will refer willingly, usually to other Elephants or into Elephant associations. The owner would need to attend all the meetings and be the primary follow-up, and new business would take time.

2. Cats by definition must have other freight providers as the company does not have all their business. The unseating of an incumbent supplier could be difficult, and if the company only had part of their business the request for referral would be hit and miss. If they respected the company enough to refer it, they would probably be using it for all their business.

3. There is no time to build the relationship with Kittens to a level that would generate new leads.

With that logic they were left with Tigers, the category the sales team was most wary of. But with a lot of persuasion, the following strategy for conducting **VALUE** Encounters with Tigers was tabled.

1. You have all these customers' business, or at least you think you do, so there is likely to be a level of mutual respect.

2. By showing interest in their business (which is the essence of a **VALUE** Encounter) reciprocity will be created.

3. The sales representative can conduct the **VALUE** Encounter meetings without the boss or a buddy, meaning they can hold a large number of meetings quickly.

4. If the **VALUE** Meeting is effective reciprocity will be created, with the next step logically being referrals to new potential clients.

They asked, 'Referral to whom?'

This was where they needed to think laterally, take the time to understand their business relationships and to categorise their Relationship DNA under the wider categories of Elephant, Tiger, Cat and Kitten. Engaging an independent firm (like **nem** in this case) helps to make this a quick and objective process.

Bill answered, 'To customers or suppliers of your customers, which you already pick up from or drop off to.'

They finally connected with the **nem** thinking!! All we had to do then was create the **VALUE** Meeting Framework. Before that happened, we prepared a Customer Services/Products Grid (CSG). Unlike professional services or financial services firms, our CSG required the company to identify the specific types of freight for each company, the movement of that freight and the largest pick-up and drop-off destinations. This required some work from each of the sales representatives and exposed their **BLIND SPOTS** quite starkly.

Their systems were also put under the microscope, as the sales representatives questioned aspects of their CSG reports that they did not understand or that did not align with their understanding of the business with each specific customer. The CSG did not have to be totally accurate; it just needed to be representative. The process of completing it caused the sales representatives to have a fresh understanding of the business they were doing with each tiger Tiger client. Our intervention and guidance prevented the process going off the rails.

The **VALUE** Meeting was a relatively straightforward exercise but covered the usual critical elements.

GREET: Normal rapport building; then transition to…

Greet

POSITION: the meeting: 'I just wanted to touch base to see how your business was going in the current climate and appreciate the time to do this face to face.' 'Our business has been hit pretty hard since the GFC with volumes down everywhere.'

Position

Then transition to **VALUE**:

VISION:	How has your business been affected?
ASK:	Only open questions
LISTEN:	Genuinely; maintain eye contact. Do not be distracted and do not interject. As the freight guys understood it, 'Just shut up and listen,' which is very hard to do for some sales people.
UNDERSTAND:	What is being said; and if we don't, ask an open question: 'When you say you were affected pretty badly, what do you mean?'– But only when appropriate!
EMPATHISE:	Show we care; in this case by saying, 'We really do understand as we are in a very similar position,' or 'That's really great, but we haven't been as clever as you.'
NEXT STEPS:	The four sales representatives did some role-playing before being sent out to conduct their **VALUE** Meetings.

Next Step

'In the current climate we really are focused on generating new volume and some new accounts. Given our relationship, would it be possible to be referred to two or three of your suppliers or customers? – When I say refer, I mean a proper introduction. It would be greatly appreciated and would help us enormously.'

Very few customers talked about better rates. The referrals were instantaneous: nearly 40% of customers immediately directed more business to the freight company. This was mostly business from sites or divisions within the businesses that the freight company had not been aware of. Some 10% of the referrals were to related group entities, and the balance to suppliers and customers, as requested. Of the 120 customers visited, over 10% provided at least one referral, 75% gave two or three, and 50% gave four or more.

The initial **VALUE** Meeting gave way to meetings with referred businesses, and the priorities morphed. Soon the sales reps' days consisted of **VALUE** Meetings, both with existing Tiger clients and with businesses those Tigers had referred them to.

The **VALUE** Meetings with the new businesses were essentially the same structure, with the following important differences.

POSITION the Meeting

'I was talking with Bob from Fasta Delivery about how the financial crisis had knocked our business around and asked for a referrals given he was happy with our services, and Bob suggested meeting with you, seeing as we already pick up/drop off to you for them. So thank you for taking the time to meet with me.'

Then Transition to VALUE

Vision: How have you found things?

Ask, Listen, Understand and Empathise did not really change.

Next Steps

'If there was an opportunity to quote for some of your work it would be greatly appreciated.'

'I am sure we would be very competitive as we already pick up and drop off to you now.'

'Is there a possibility we could be given an opportunity?'

These **VALUE** Meetings were recorded and reported back to the owner weekly as part of the normal sales meeting.

It took one week before the company secured additional work from existing customers, and two weeks before the first referral resulted in the opening of a new account. Within ten weeks there was a noticeable increase in sales revenue, and after four months it was obvious that the decline of the previous nine months had been reversed, with sustained activity returning to the $9 million annualised level achieved before the financial crisis.

6. It Is Not About Selling

The **VALUE** Encounter Methodology works because the interaction is a non-sales approach. The process of engaging has commercial objectives – we want to sell our products or services – but the **VALUE** Encounter ensures that the first step is not seen as selling. Instead, it leverages the relationship and creates reciprocity.

We Are Sick of Being Sold To!

When we say the **VALUE** Encounter is counterintuitive, we mean it is different from what the client expects us to do. If we are in a business development role, most clients expect us to be pushing or selling our products and services, which is perfectly understandable. But in today's business environment we are tired of being sold to. We can efficiently access most things we want for ourselves. The internet has changed the way we buy.

For instance, there is anecdotal evidence that so many homebuyers use internet searches that over 90% of them have already decided whether or not they will purchase a property that they visit. This has major ramifications for real estate agents. Their role is no longer to sell the benefits and features of the property but to understand what appeals to the prospective purchaser. Their role moves towards reinforcing the buyer's decision or suggesting alternative properties that better meet their needs.

We Switch Quickly

Because we are bombarded with information we have also become experts at filtering out information. We know we can search or Google most things we are interested in, so when we are confronted with traditional sales approaches, we switch off very quickly. Even cognitive (i.e. needs-based) sales approaches are treated with suspicion, and when a sale is attempted our suspicion is confirmed and we switch off. This is often in the first minute of the conversation.

CHAPTER 9

Guaranteed Sales

CHAPTER 9

....

Guaranteed Sales

While the VALUE Encounter Methodology had been successfully applied at the freight company; and any other businesses for that matter, hardened sales focused organisations failed to quickly embrace the approach.

'We do that anyway' was routinely explained by any seasoned sales executives; 'Relationships are already the key to our sales effort' and a myriad of other responses from impatient sales professionals meant the VALUE Encounter Methodology was rarely adopted by businesses that already had a deep and traditional sales culture.

There had to be a better way to deploy the VALUE Encounter Methodology through a far wider range of businesses and industries.

The answer came from deploying the methodology as the 'execution' phase of a laser-focused sales effort.

With two **nem** Partners devotion to the exercise a range of highly sophisticated approaches were redeployed under a simple framework that would appeal to even the most hardened sales organisation.

cama™ was Born

That framework is named **cama**™ and it brings a robust quantitative and qualitative framework to the often subjective approach adopted for identifying sales growth opportunities.

The process firstly identifies the business's Competitive Advantage, then identifies the most Attractive Markets/Segments in which to grow revenue, and then independently validates these against competitors and other industry benchmarks.

The **cama**™ Program comprises **FOUR** stages.

1. Stakeholder Discovery Session

cama™ commences with a client-facing stakeholder workshop that identifies the businesses most critical aspects of their Competitive Advantage and existing and potential Market or Segments that the business sees as Attractive.

Competitive Advantage

Is identified by documenting the seven most important criteria that determine the competitive advantage of each product or service. The first two criteria or factors are mandatory; Price and Relationships. The other five are brainstormed and agreed amongst the team.

That team are the management team and the client-facing personnel. Once the seven criteria are identified they are then weighted against each other out of one hundred. This can be a challenging process and because the stakeholders are present, including the Chief Executive and/ or the owners, it is critical that the workshop is facilitated by a capable independent facilitator.

Once they have navigated their way through the challenges of agreeing what the other five competitive advantages are, the next challenge is the weightings and their ratings against each one.

The views, opinions and input of all parties needs to be balanced and moderated so a true representation of the businesses competitive advantage is documented and agreed.

Examples of the most common Competitive Advantage criteria are as follows:

> Price (Mandatory)
> Relationship (Mandatory)
> Experience
> Speciality
> Quality
> Service
> Reputation
> Functionality
> Emotive

Having gained consensus, the next challenge is to rate the businesses performance against each of the seven criteria, by each major product or service offering. This grading is out of five. Five using whole numbers only has been found to be highly effective. It is not possible to sit on the fence with a grading of one to five. Two is below-midpoint of satisfactory and three above-midpoints, with Five representing the most favourable and One the least for each criteria.

Once again, facilitation plays a vital role, particularly where there are multiple discreet product and service offerings.

Market Attractiveness

Having documented and agreed the competitive advantage criteria, weighting and rating, the stakeholder group is then asked to identify all the market segments that they operate in and all those that they desire to operate in with their *existing* products and services.

cama™ is not the appropriate framework for exploring new product or service offerings as there is no existing customer experience. The launch of new products or services is the domain of more traditional strategic assessments and analysis; which is not the domain of the **cama**™ framework.

cama™'s objective is to maximise sales growth for existing, known products and services. For most businesses, the segments can be quite effectively identified prior to the workshop so as not waste the entire stakeholder group's time BUT the workshop needs to tease out any additional market segments that the stakeholder group believe will represent opportunities for growth.

The five criteria are not variable. They are accepted, well established criteria that are applied widely and accepted globally as the five critical market assessment criteria.

They are as follows:

> Market Size
> Market Growth
> Profit Margin
> Competitive Intensity
> Location

These criteria can be validated by accessing independent data and information which exists in the public domain or by accessing subscriber research and even independently commissioned research where necessary.

The next challenge is to rate the businesses attractiveness to each market or segment against each of the five criteria, by each major product or service offering. Once again, this grading is out of five with One being least attractive and Five being most attractive.

2. Research Phase

Having identified weighted and graded the seven competitive advantage criteria, and five market advantage criteria for each product or service, the next phase of **cama**™ is to independently validate the stakeholder assessments.

cama™ *is then Validated*

In relation to the competitive advantage criteria, this requires feedback directly from the customers or purchasers of the businesses products or services. This is a critical phase and must be representative of the entire customer list (or market). To achieve this there must be a proportion who are randomly selected or identified.

Those that are identified are communicated with as valued customers or prospective customers, are asked to participate by agreeing to discuss their experiences with the business consultants either over the phone or in person.

They are asked to grade the same seven criteria, relative to their experiences with other suppliers of the same services or products. They are then asked one or two open questions to determine if there should be any other criteria or any other important facts affecting their decision to buy the products or services in question. More importantly, WHY they like or dislike buying from the business in question.

The market segments and industries are then independently researched via access to available industry data, subscribed industry information (such as IBIS) and from subject matter experts.

This is usually a very illuminating process; competitive advantage is a relative thing after all AND often the lure of new market segments clouds the real opportunities that exist within existing markets and for that matter, existing customers.

3. Feedback Phase

The research findings are collated, analysed and assessed and presented back to the stakeholders in a facilitated workshop format. Through group discussion the Competitive Advantage criteria are reweighted and the most Attractive Market segments are agreed.

This is a critical session that provides many insights and usually runs for half the time that was applied to the discovery workshop conducted during phase one.

At the completion of this feedback session the business has a clear Competitive positioning statement that has emanated from their customer base AND a very clear understanding of where their Competitive Advantage can best be deployed in terms of target markets or segments.

This can be presented numerically and graphically and can completely align sales activities and priorities. The following is an example of how one of the firm's clients realigned their sales focus.

cama™ *then Realigns Sales Activities*

The business we will highlight here is a medium-sized engineering firm that operates regionally and specialises in making customised engineering parts and importing and distributing standard stock items primarily to the coal industry that exports and to the power generation industry that utilises coal to generate power.

Both sectors (coal and power generation) had been privatised some years ago and were subjected to significant disruption as new overseas owners took control of the operations. This created significant supply disruptions and the realignment of some parts to overseas suppliers. Volume losses occurred and together with the stagnant industry outlook a concerted effort had been undertaken by the company to move into other industries.

Water, primarily irrigation, and heavy rail had been targeted for some eighteen months. Water was relatively new to the company while they had considerable knowledge of heavy rail due to their supply to the coal industry.

The following represents the change in focus that occurred as a result of the **cama**™ workshops, research and feedback phases.

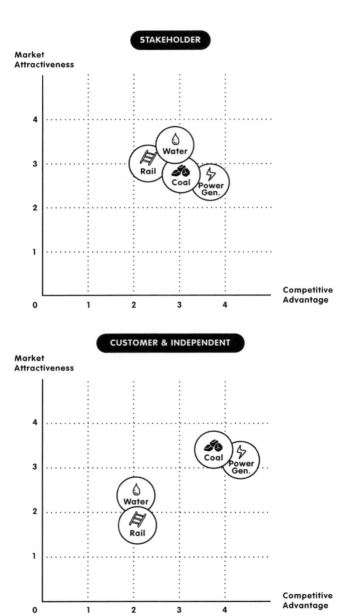

This **cama**™ program identified, and quantified both numerically and graphically that the company *should be placing much more emphasis on the sectors in which they already competed and leverage far deeper into those sectors, educating procurement of their unique competitive advantage which was bespoke, service and efficiency* INSTEAD of dedicating resources and energy into chasing new markets that had little synergistic benefits and were unlikely to succeed.

The business's Competitive Advantage was heavily weighted to its bespoke custom solutions, short lead times relative to competitors while the Market Attractive highlighted that their two largest existing markets were not contracting as quickly as they had determined and that there was opportunity to grow sales through clever import replacement programs across a wider range of divisions within each of their existing customers.

In addition, the gas industry was identified as having almost identical Market Attractiveness as it was expanding, was geographically aligned with coal and power generation and was already a very large industry.

Heavy rail was dominated by three major companies making meaningful penetration difficult and water was geographically spread making connectivity inefficient and expensive.

Having realigned the businesses focus the next phase was executing **cama**™ - the fourth phase.

4. Execution Phase

Having realigned the direction of the sales function to those segments that offer the most attractive returns, and are aligned with the company's 'relative' competitive advantages, the business development program was then established by mapping all existing business relationships in those segments being targeted.

Rather than cold call on prospects, the existing networks were leveraged by using the VALUE Encounter Methodology and creating connectivity and sales opportunities.

cama™ *VALUE Encounters*

The businesses relationships were identified as Elephants, Tigers, Cats and Kittens and the following strategies put in place.

Elephants

These were predominantly the two owners' relationships with industry participants and the company's field engineers' relationships with their customer's maintenance engineers.

The field engineers in particular, were asked to check off a number of prepared open questions with their Elephant client relationships while on site. No overt contact activity to be undertaken – just a VALUE Meeting framework at the next time of contact. One aspect of the VALUE Meeting was to identify if any other departments purchased similar parts or components. Another was to ask what were their biggest frustrations in relation to suppliers of similar products. This question was asked with the confidence that they knew they were quicker in turnarounds, could provide solutions to tricky problems and they were priced competitively with other suppliers, particularly those that imported.

The owners were also trained in how to more widely position the direction of the business within the industry segments they were operating and mixing with socially; and were the primary source of follow up when the field engineers came back with the names of people in other divisions that were worthy of making contact with.

Tigers

Once again most were at the engineering and maintenance level and a similar approach was adopted to that with Elephants, however a number of Tigers were identified for overt contact via VALUE Calls to set up 'How is business going VALUE Meetings.'

Cats

Contact strategy around brand repositioning, regional promotion and electronic connectivity deployed to increase awareness. Actively looking for personal connectivity through Elephants and Tigers.

Kittens

Similar to Cats.

cama™ *Generates Success Quickly*

The immediate and positive outcome of applying **cama**™ was the alignment of all the stakeholders of the business on the primary growth segments and customers within them.

The mandate for each stakeholder is clear, unambiguous but does require them to focus and report on specific VALUE Encounters.

In this application the business obtained immediate additional sales orders from existing customers for parts and repairs in areas where they were previously not considered a viable supplier.

The business also went on to develop supply arrangements with several other divisions within their existing customers and also set about developing an import replacement program on time critical parts and infrastructure.

As accreditation, or certification, was being secured to supply parts and service into the gas industry connections into that market were also identified and contact strategies developed for future VALUE Meetings when ready.

While the business did not have any customers in the gas sector at the commencement of the **cama** program, the Execution phase identified many deep relationships into the industry.

One of the first VALUE Meetings by the sales executive leading the business development initiatives into the industry obtained a referral from a Relationship in the coal industry to a procurement manager in a large gas production company.

His Relationship made a personal introduction and a genuine VALUE Meeting one on one with the procurement manager was expected. When he arrived he was greeted by the party to whom he was introduced, had a brief discussion in the foyer, and was then lead into a small auditorium where twenty-five colleagues had gathered to hear about the unique qualities of the business.

Not only had the business been introduced, its unique competitive advantage had been conveyed and all the maintenance engineers and procurement specialists had been gathered to hear how the business had assisted their coal industry customers to improve their maintenance regimes, reduce stock holdings and improve supply lead times.

It certainly was not a cold call...........!!!!

This business went on to experience double digit sales growth quarter on quarter with similar improvements in profitability, and this was in the industries and with the customers that they had previously considered mature and in decline.

cama™ *provided the sales force with the messaging, the facts, focus and confidence to implement VALUE Encounters with laser accuracy that resulted in rapid and sustained improvements in sales and profitability.*

CHAPTER 10

Value-Added Outcomes

CHAPTER 10

....

Value-Added Outcomes

The firm's unique approach combined with **cama**™ have consistently provided outstanding Value-Added Outcomes for the clients of the firm. Here are a few other examples that demonstrate the breadth and depth of the process.

1. The Window Cleaner

Having done the research, accepted the risks and set up the business, we were all pretty gung ho about the future and ready for some seriously interesting challenges.

Then came one of the first genuine referrals to an actual business owner. That referral came to me and, as I listened to the accountant explaining that one of his clients was nearing retirement with no clear pathways out of his business and could do with a fresh set of eyes, I was getting pretty excited.

Then came the crunch, it was a dad, son and mum window cleaning business turning over $300,000 a year. My excitement evaporated as I sat deflated with the prospect that my career had sunk to this level.

As my colleagues reminded me, it was, however, a referral from an accountant that had many other clients. While the coffee meeting was probably going to be a waste of time, if it was important to the accountant it should be important to me.

So, I took down the details and made contact and the coffee meeting was scheduled for the end of the week, in the evening, after the work for the day was complete.

When the meeting eventuated, it was in the family home and it was immediately clear that these were genuine hard-working people, with genuine issues and were failing to see how they could sell their business.

While the son worked in the business as a window cleaner he had no interest in taking it over, particularly if he had to pay for it, and the father was so busy working the business he had no idea how he was going to sell it to someone else. The mother did the books, manually! And they really appeared to be exhausted.

At the coffee meeting enough was gleaned to know that the Review process could be very beneficial in helping them to see the opportunities for them and their business.

The coffee meeting, after signing the firm's one-way confidentiality deed, revealed the business turned over only $260,000 and this was with the son cleaning six days a week, nine to ten hours a day and the father three days. The father spent the other three days a week visiting sites and preparing quotes. The mother did the invoicing, predominantly in the evening when the father and son returned with their run sheet of completed jobs.

Of the three days of quoting, few were ever followed up and the conversion rate was extremely low. Added to this, the number of calls was constant and driven by advertisements in four or five local papers and a half-page Yellow Pages ad, and online presence.

The advertising costs were well over $100,000 a year!!

I knew that there was considerable VALUE to be obtained from a comprehensive desktop review so at the conclusion of the meeting I recommended precisely that.

At a cost of $1,250, payable only if they obtained value, a desktop review was proposed and agreed and a time scheduled for the following week, once again after the day's work was finished.

The Review Commenced

The standard review was undertaken with the owner, his wife and their accountant. The son could not attend and had little interest in the process.

Over the course of the next hour and a half the following key aspects of the business and the operations were obtained:

1. The business consisted of domestic work and commercial (office and retail) work. Office and retail were predominantly suburban shopping strips and offices. Domestic was houses, single and two storey. There were no high-rise apartment blocks or office complexes.

2. Of the quotes issued, which averaged some 100 per week, only about 20% converted to actual jobs and there was no follow-up mechanism in place to follow up each quote. Conversion was based purely on the customers ringing back.

3. Of the two types of work, domestic was usually more profitable. The commercial work was more competitively priced and often involved several shop fronts in a line. Competitors would continually undercut prices to secure new work, often resulting to inefficient runs of work as one, two, three or even four shop front in the street would move periodically. The only way to prevent this occurring was to get to know the business owners, but this just made the work even more inefficient, because that meant doing the work when the owners were working. That was generally when the businesses were relatively busy, which meant even more inefficient work as people were avoided.

4. Domestic work was priced between $100 to $300 a job and the son could complete four domestic jobs a day if in the same area. Commercial work was priced between $30 and $70 with an average of fifteen jobs in a day. Based on a forty-two week year (weather often hampered work) that was an average income profile of $294,000.

5. The advertising expenditure was $120,000 which seemed very high but it was critical for lead flow, particularly domestic work.

6. The accountant confirmed that the owners paid their son $90,000 a year leaving them both with even less after operating costs which included insurance, work cover, materials administration and bookkeeping and of course the advertising costs!!

7. As the questions were worked through it became very obvious that there was no follow-up process for the quotes, based on the fact they already struggled to issue quotes, let alone follow them up. This was non-negotiable. The wife in particular would have no bar of the implied recommendation to follow up quotes. She was already overrun invoicing and chasing payments.

8. The other interesting fact was that apart from the commercial work only a small number of domestic customers were repeat customers and the business certainly had little if any record of who they were.

On conclusion of the review session which ran for ninety-five minutes we provided the owners with verbal feedback that we believed there was scope to double the profitability of the business with minimal additional effort. While this was met with some intrigue, shall we say, the owners agreed to move forward and have us complete our analysis and table our report.

Armed with the facts as outlined, and after receiving the businesses transaction listings and customer files, the answers and recommendations that followed became quite obvious. Now keep in mind, the recommendations were made before iPhones, iPads and mobile apps existed and in any event these owners were not technology savvy in any event. The wife struggled with MYOB and had no interest in doing any more than she already did.

The following were the basis of the recommendations tabled:

1. The business needed to commence to capture customer details on a customer database. Their accountant was able to provide the software and training for this which was very straightforward.

2. It was recommended that the business concentrate on domestic work, in preference to commercial work AND that this be a gradual process. When a good domestic job was secured, that was straightforward, the quote was accepted with haggling and requesting discounts for cash that owner would be asked if they would like to go on the businesses

database and be contacted at a future period for the next clean. They were asked to complete a small two-part form and tick three months, six months, nine months or twelve, and sign to agree to go on the database and to be contacted.

3.   Based on the current churn rates, the higher priced domestic pricing and the winding down of the commercial work, we estimated that the income could increase to an annualised volume of $425,000 AND that was before the owner ceased to quote.

4.   Based on the same information we estimated that it would take approximately eighteen months for the business to have sufficient recurring work so as to cease to have to quote. That time could add an additional $162,000 in revenue if it was applied to domestic work.

5.   Additionally, with the necessity to quote reduced to negligible levels the business would save the majority of the $120,000 in advertising expenditure.

Here were owners so caught up in the whirlwind of doing what they were doing they could no longer look at their business objectively.

This simple review identified life-changing opportunities if they could implement the simple recommendations. A lot would rest with the son coming on board and assisting with the process.

Their accountant was very helpful and we stayed in touch as the business gradually transformed itself from a constant churn to a recurring service business with a large list of domestic customers.

As it turned out, it took only nine months to no longer be relying on quoting and with that the advertising costs were slashed and the Yellow Pages contract was not renewed. The son worked five days and the father three days and the accountant took over the bookkeeping service from the wife of the owner. With that came a more streamlined payment process and an improvement in cash flow on an annualised revenue base of $430,000. The son went on to buy the business, on vendor terms, and to further expand the business into an increasing number of a joining suburbs.

While the initial referral to such a small business was met with a degree of disappointment, the process itself was extremely powerful in relation to obtaining the owners engagement and identifying substantial benefits that were not obvious on the surface. The following nine months provided one of the most satisfying business experiences we had ever had. Life-changing for them and for us... as we gained the confidence to work with any business, irrespective of size and complexity.

2. The Accounting Software Company

The accounting software company referred to earlier engaged **nem** to undertake a comprehensive review of their business. As previously outlined, the review confirmed the Managing Director's opinion that the company could charge their customer base substantially more than their existing maintenance fees for the upgraded version of their software, which was due for release. His entire management team, however, was sceptical and expressed grave concern for the business' future should a charge be applied.

There were several thousand businesses using their software which paid only modest monthly maintenance fees. Nearly all customers had purchased their software at some point in the past. An added complication was an embedded dealer channel network, some of which supported other products. They received a portion of the maintenance fee for maintaining the relationship and supporting the software. The dealer network also supported their clients with training and was protective of their relationships. They too were highly sceptical and suspicious of the software company's intentions.

The review highlighted that the additional functionality of the new version was so significant that not only could it be charged for through a higher maintenance fee, but the dealers could also benefit from the compulsory nature of the upgrade by charging all their customers to install it. A further charge was available from the extensive training of users due to the substantial increases in functionality.

While the Managing Director could see this, his management team could not, at least not until the firm's approach or '**nem** Way' was commenced.

The **nem** review was the first step to bringing the company into the **UNKNOWN**. The subsequent market assessment, trials and pilot upgrades removed resistance, opened up knowledge of the company's customer base, and resulted in a seamless rollout of the upgrade.

The software company's revenue increased by over 60%, with a material portion falling to the bottom line. The dealers enjoyed higher commissions of similar proportions and the company accelerated the payment cycle to dealers by one month, creating a one-off cash injection for all dealers. The dealers were also occupied for a considerable period of time in training and installing, which resulted in fully recovered consultancy fees.

This was a copybook outcome. The firm had developed a unique software product. Their software was uniquely positioned in the market. It was more robust and functional than off-the-shelf packages and was far more affordable and easier to install than other available solutions. It was the ideal software for a large number of growing small to medium enterprises.

The Managing Director could see a significant opportunity in the market for the software, but whenever a sales opportunity emerged the company was dragged into a traditional sales process, and the conversion process was very slow.

Two of the firm's partners were engaged by the company to develop a **VALUE** Encounter engagement process for selling their accounting software. This was a real challenge, as traditional sales approaches did not necessarily evolve from a referral: usually an approached company would respond by presenting a systems specification, which was provided to a variety of vendors to pitch for. Even more challenging was that the people judging the pitches were rarely systems experts and could not objectively assess what was being presented to them.

This was particularly relevant to companies that had outgrown their off-the-shelf packages. They were typically growing, but did not yet have a qualified accountant on staff and relied on a competent bookkeeper and their accounting firm to prepare formal accounts and their tax returns.

When the firm undertook the **VALUE** Encounter review it quickly realised that the traditional way of selling was so entrenched that once a company started looking for accounting software the process became protracted and inefficient, often spanning several months. If the company was to secure a large number of new sites it had to identify businesses that could benefit from buying its software *but were not yet looking*. The challenge was set. The company agreed – so much they contracted one of our partners full time.

The significance of such a challenge cannot be underestimated as the business owners of the target market were not aware that they needed upgraded accounting software. This was not an area that was high on their agendas.

As the Managing Director once quipped, 'If I don't want to talk to the person next to me on a long flight I tell them I sell accounting software.'

Undeterred, the **VALUE** Encounter review was conducted, considerable research of the target market undertaken and the firm's networks tapped into. This uncovered a number of facts and exposed the typical sales process that evolved when businesses did in fact upgrade to competitors' products.

1. **The gap was indeed extremely large.**

    An estimated 200,000 businesses had outgrown their off-the-shelf accounting packages. To put this in perspective, the business had several thousand existing clients and could quadruple the turnover of their business by doubling this to 10,000.

2. **There were very few referrals.**

    Even if their advisors, such as accountants, knew their clients could benefit from more sophisticated accounting software, they were reluctant to get involved.

3. **The traditional sales process was flawed.**

    Once a business started to look at new accounting software, the process was usually driven by non-technical people, who struggled to evaluate the alternatives effectively.

4. **Implementation was disruptive and costly.**

    Alternative vendors would portray their systems as straightforward and simple to implement, even when they were very sophisticated and required specific expertise, and even the re-engineering of aspects of the business's processes. This invariably resulted in time delays and cost overruns when these systems were chosen.

5. **The benefits rarely materialised.**

    Often the considerable cost of the system was justified by improved efficiencies and functionality, usually the result of improved systems functionality and automating many of the manual tasks in the business.

    If not implemented extremely well, with effective staff training, the functionality proposed rarely materialised. In some cases, the implementation process actually put the business at risk.

6. **The owners were not involved.**

    Where there were accounting systems upgrades, the business owners were rarely involved in their selection and implementation. They often delegated these processes to their internal accounting staff, sometimes supported by an independent consultant to manage the specification and selection criteria.

    Owners' involvement was usually relegated to final approval and signing the very large cheque.

7. **Business owners' objectives were counterproductive.**

    They often centred on improving revenue, generating improved profitability and creating long-term value from their businesses.

    Accounting systems were seen as a central overhead, important but still a cost to the business.

8. **Ignorance was bliss.**

    Business owners did not know that systematic improvements in their business systems and processes could generate considerable improvements in profitability, sales and free cash flow, whether these were manual or computerised.

    For example, a business has specified trading terms, which are usually listed on the invoice. When the month-end statements are mailed, the balance is listed as current, thirty, sixty, or ninety days. Our client had found that listing Current and Overdue only increased collection by 15%.

We found literally dozens of tips and examples that if implemented could improve the profitability, sales and cash flow of just about any business.

History Repeats Itself

The previously **UNKNOWN** was exposed – adding value in relation to systems and processes did not necessarily rely on upgrading accounting systems. Business owners could benefit significantly from improving little things that they did every day; they just needed to know how. The review highlighted about fifty tips and tactics, and we knew there were many more. In order to identify them, all we needed to unlock was the knowledge within the company's network of employees, dealers and clients.

Like any major project that succeeds, this one was led by the Managing Director and owner. Within a few weeks the company had identified over 700 business systems improvements that could significantly improve performance regardless of which system a business was using. Some improvements could only be achieved through automation and some were unique to the company's software; but the vast majority were there for the picking for just about any business that chose to adopt them.

Over the next few months the 700 business improvements were reviewed, edited, tested and documented into a published guide. This Business Improvement Guide (BIG) was the first **VALUE**-add, an ideal engagement confirmation giveaway to business owners and their advisors.

The objective was to obtain specific engagements where BIG could be handed out to attendees in exchange for their business cards and the agreement to meet with a company representative.

The initial pilots were so successful it became apparent that the follow-up meetings needed to be able to rely on a systematic series of steps that delivered genuine **VALUE**, whichever the path they took. They needed to be efficient **VALUE** Encounters so as not to waste each other's time and to leave a positive impression; and if, and only if, there was a genuine need for, a systems upgrade assessment, the correct commercial pathway was recommended.

If this lead generation activity was scalable, the number of leads for the company's accounting software installations might be very large. With this in mind, the company and the **nem** team, created their unique **VALUE** Encounter approach of selling.

The Company's VALUE Encounter was Born

This process of selling turned the traditional business systems sales process of several months into several weeks. The conversion rate of the traditional sales process had been 10%. With the **VALUE** Encounter it was over 70%.

Like any **VALUE** Encounter, their approach relied on a complementary coffee meeting with a prospective client. Whether that meeting was generated by the free copy of the BIG, a referral or from the use of their free online scorecard, it was always a **VALUE** Meeting. Its primary objective was to determine if the company's business systems could genuinely benefit the business and, if they could, whether the business owner was interested.

If there was no genuine prospect of the system meeting their immediate needs, the meeting investigated alternative paths they might pursue:

- Improving the system they were already using, functionally and operationally, and staying with it (e.g. MYOB, QuickBooks, etc.)
- Migrating to a more suitable low-end solution (like XERO)
- Considering the big migration path to a full Enterprise Solution (ERP).

All with a recommendation to a trusted third party if applicable.
If their software was a good potential fit, the next step was to determine how good a fit it was, and what benefits could be delivered. With this objective the company developed a Business Systems Assessment tool and an online Scorecard Assessment. Depending on the sophistication and complexity of the business, the coffee meeting would recommend applying either one or both of the tools.

The tools were developed to efficiently determine the scale of benefits the business could enjoy from upgrading their existing accounting software to the company's. The tools very conservatively quantified the benefits in terms of sales revenue, profit and overall free cash flow. If the business owner expressed a desire to realise these benefits, the next step was to seek their agreement to a Scope of Works, which they needed to pay for!

Scope of Works

Unlike a traditional 'scope of works' for new business systems, their Scope of Works concentrates solely on existing areas of operation and functionality, and on identified business improvement objectives. It is *never* to include bells and whistles: existing areas of operation, functionality and business improvements only! For example, if the business had a manual stock replenishment system where a staff member monitored stock levels through spreadsheets or physical verification, the Scope of Works would specify only that basic, perpetual stock system and mastering its use.

Added sophistication could come later, once core functionality was operating effectively. This was because a typical systems implementation covers several areas of a business: accounting, invoicing and debtors, accounts payable, payroll, inventory and fixed assets. It is challenging for any organisation to undergo a systems upgrade and learn how to use the new system to replicate their manual tasks. To burden them with additional functionality at that time creates an exponential level of difficulty.

If their software was to be implemented quickly and generate benefits, it had to be as seamless as possible. The Scope of Works was critical to ensuring the system was not over-specified and could be installed quickly, with as little disruption and risk to the business as possible.

This was a genuinely unique approach. It delivered rapid conversion in comparison to traditional vendor sales methods and also created VALUE irrespective of the sales outcome for the company.

As a consequence, a continual stream of referrals from the VALUE Encounters evolved from a large proportion of businesses that benefited from the guidance and direction they received during the initial VALUE Meeting.

There were also frequent surprises from the approach adopted.

I Want Your Software!

One that was particularly relevant to the strength of the approach was a referral by a banker to the company. The business was a client of the bank and had an out-of-date accounting system and were considering moving.

The banker had arranged for their client to receive the Business Improvement Guide and the client then rang the software company!

A coffee meeting with the accountant of the business was organised to find out if the software was a reasonable fit.

Before the Business Development (BD) specialist could ask some of the normal questions in relation to the business, the accountant indicated that they were happy to proceed straight away to a paid Scope of Works.

Surprised but undeterred, the BD specialist asked if they minded answering a few questions to determine the size and scope of the potential installation.

As it turned out, while the business had a substantial turnover, the vast majority of sales were to a handful of overseas customers who were invoiced weekly, and in some cases monthly.

In addition, the product produced was powdered milk that was sold in bulk. The customers of the company then converted the milk into packaged products in each of their respective markets.

With such small transaction levels and simple stock holdings, their accounting software would have been a major overkill and would not generate any meaningful benefits to the business, would add additional costs and create considerable disruption if all data and files needed to be converted.

Based on this information, the BD specialist recommended that they upgrade their existing off-the-shelf software and provided the name of a trusted vendor whom they would personally introduce.

You cannot win them all… but the right advice, added real VALUE.

The accountant was very appreciative and thanked the BD specialist sincerely and then offered to provide a quick tour of the plant before leaving which was gratefully accepted.

On with the fluoro vest, hair net and white cap and off they went. The BD specialist was surprised to see the size of the operation.

The plant was sophisticated and there were quite a few employees who the BD specialist found spanned seven days around the clock.

The plant needed to keep up with two deliveries of milk a day and was running at full capacity.

When the BD specialist enquired about the challenges that were caused by these factors, the accountant explained that the business could not increase capacity without massive capital expenditure.

As a result, maintenance windows were restricted to an eight-hour window on Sundays AND the rostering and management of the workforce was critical.

With this information, the BD specialist became immediately confident that their payroll module and fixed asset module could be of enormous benefit.

So the question of which software they used for payroll and fixed assets was asked. The accountant explained that they used the same off-the-shelf accounting package for payroll and they had no specialist fixed asset module, just Excel spreadsheets as feeders for journal entries into the accounting ledger.

With that news, the potential VALUE of adopting a more sophisticated payroll system and a dedicated fixed asset module were discussed and a Scope of Works proposed.

The accountant agreed to proceed and pay for the Scope which was undertaken a week later.

That Scope highlighted the benefit of monitoring and scheduling maintenance with constant reminders. It also highlighted the efficiencies and the time savings associated with paying their 300-odd employees with a more automated and efficient payroll system.

The business went on to install the new payroll and fixed asset modules while retaining their existing accounting software for general ledger purposes.

This was a genuine win–win situation resulting in the accounting software company obtaining a new client for payroll and fixed assets, and a very happy accountant that did not need to go through the process of changing accounting systems.

Scaling Reciprocity!!!

From this genuine commercial engagement came the most unlikely referral. While the initial referral to the accounting software company came from the business's banker, they did not know the banker, either in name or in person.

So it was with some surprise that a month or so after installing the payroll and fixed asset modules the software company received a call from the business's banker asking to meet.

The meeting proceeded and after the initial pleasantries the banker said… 'It has been some time since a client has given such a glowing reference to accounting software vendor… in fact it has never happened in my twenty years of banking.'

The banker went on to say that having an important client talk so positively about them prompted him to improve his understanding of their software and to understand the approach they had adopted, because they had many hundreds of clients that need to improve their reporting but they did not know where to turn.

This approach resulted in the General Manager becoming involved in the discussion and tempering the natural sales instincts of the BD specialist who saw the next year's budget being achieved in a blink.

The General Manager understood the significance of the opportunity, an opportunity to obtain a very large number of leads to prospective new clients! But this was a major bank, with many staff with their own priorities and key performance indicators against which they were judged and remunerated.

If they needed to build relationships across the entire bank it would overwhelm their resources. They needed to develop a referral mechanism that the individual business bankers would buy into, that helped them to meet their performance criteria and was a win, win for all stakeholders.

The General Manager undertook a very good VALUE Meeting and found that the most pressing challenge for the bankers in the field was winning over new business.

In the context of this challenge, while existing clients with poor systems were a logical referral to them, the banker already banked those clients.

The real frustration for the business bankers was when they had a new prospect that they had worked on for some time that could not produce reliable information quickly enough, or in the format required by the bank, to assess their suitability for the bank.

The opportunity became clear to the General Manager so he asked the logical next open question... 'As a start how do you think we could assist your bankers to get those prospects over the line?'

The answer was a program of introducing prospective clients early in the banks' business development process to assist with an independent assessment of their accounting and reporting systems. No obligation, no cost, but with an assurance that they were very likely able to assist, if by only pointing the business in the right direction.

3. The Stock Feed Company

While the firm grew its reputation amongst a wide network of private business and their associated service providers each of the partners had much wider networks.

With the majority of partners having come from senior corporate backgrounds those networks spanned the highest echelons of business.

It was no surprise therefore to receive referrals from the top end of town and that is precisely what happened to one of the partners. A message was left at the office from an old contact that was a non-executive Director on the Board of a publicly listed agricultural business.

After ringing her contact back, the referral was to the newly appointed Managing Director of the company who was based in Melbourne. With the Head Office in Sydney, the new Managing Director was looking to justify the relocation of the Head Office operations to Melbourne and needed an analysis, justification and cost assessment to be completed.

Having run a major division of the company for the past four years that was based in Melbourne, the Managing Director was looking to move all non-board functions such as finance, human resources, corporate services and projects to Melbourne. But this needed to be thoroughly assessed as the move needed to be justified before being tabled to the Board for approval.

Having been briefed quite thoroughly over the phone an appointment was made by the **nem** partner to meet the Managing Director to agree the scope and the terms of the project.

A very polite meeting took place and after much discussion and clarification of the scope a fee of $60,000 was proposed. The meeting immediately lost its convivial feel as the Managing Director raised his voice and said; 'I am not paying that... You referred to me because you are not a top tier consulting firm and that is a top tier fee.'

After a brief and low-key explanation by the **nem** partner of the time that would be required to be applied and that there were probably going to need to be third party research reports to substantiate the cost savings the Managing Director calmed down and a more pragmatic discussion followed.

The **nem** partner asked what level of fees would be acceptable for which a fee of $30,000 was put forward. With that fee tabled the **nem** partner agreed to the fee provided the company provided unrestricted access to the information required and to the people within Head Office AND provided there was a right to recover preapproved third-party costs that exceeded $7,500.

On that basis the Managing Director agreed to a fixed fee of $30,000, winner take all (his words!) and promptly asked when could the project commence.

As it turned out the **nem** partner was in Sydney the following day and agreed she could rearrange appointments so as to commence the next morning. They shook hands on the deal, agreed to sign an engagement letter the next time they met and agreed to commence.

It Is Never As It Appears On The Surface!!

At 8.30 am the next morning the **nem** partner appeared at the Head Office reception in Sydney to be greeted by a Head Office executive who was tasked with coordinating the review within the Head Office.

After a briefing and a list of required information agreed the Head Office executive went off to obtain the information while the **nem** partner commenced the interviews with Head Office staff.

Everyone was very cooperative and understood the nature of the review, particularly the Finance Director. He was quite candid about the office moving as a fait accompli which was strange given that the move was not yet approved and there were many aspects to such a move that needed to be understood before approval could occur at Board level.

Further questioning revealed the Finance Director was leaving in a few weeks, having accepted a package after being unsuccessful in his application for the Managing Director's role. Something just didn't sit right but the **nem** partner could not put her figure on it.

Numbers Rarely Lie!

It was not until early in the afternoon that things started to fall into place when the actual Head Office costs were analysed against budget, the prior year and more importantly the analysts forecasts. While the costs incurred were no higher than the prior year they were well above budget and even exceeded the guidance to analysts.

When the information was presented to the Finance Director the explanation was simple: 'They appointed a Melbourne-based Managing Director so there are no more Sydney Head Office costs, they are now in the Melbourne Divisions' books. They have an office there already and much of the infrastructure needed is there. It is as simple as that.'

To be fair to the Finance Director, there were a lot of changes occurring at the time. Businesses were being sold and bought and there was general uncertainty after appointing an internal Melbourne-based candidate into the Managing Director's role BUT it did not take the **nem** partner long to join the many dots to conclude that the new Managing Director's Head Office costs had been incorrectly compiled by the Finance Director.

Shortly after summarising the situation the Managing Director called to see how things were going and to let the **nem** partner know he was in Sydney the next day. After a brief conversation the **nem** partner suggested they meet and a chat over breakfast was agreed.

Over breakfast the **nem** partner tabled the numbers and analysis and went onto to explain that from a budget perspective there were no Sydney Head Office costs to save. They had been cut out of the budget and unless they were in his former Division's budget, actual costs were running above budget and analysts' projections!!!!

You could have heard a pin drop!!!

From that moment on the scope of the engagement changed enormously with the **nem** partner really only assisting with the Managing Director's Board presentation and making sure the financial facts in the presentation were supported with the appropriate reports and analysis should the headline numbers be questioned during the meeting.

VALUE Can Occur In Many Ways!

Two weeks later the Managing Director called the **nem** partner to thank her for her assistance and to advise that the move was approved and revised budgets adopted by the Board. A great outcome and the Managing Director asked the **nem** partner to pop in to chat further and to bring the Engagement Letter (which still had not been signed) and the bill.

This duly occurred and it was a cordial meeting that was brief and to the point.

As the **nem** partner was walking back to the office the Managing Director called her and said: 'I have just opened the invoice to approve and it is only for $12,000, I expected a bill for $30,000 and am happy to pay it.' With that the **nem** partner said; 'Yes we had agreed a fixed fee of $30,000 winner take all but I would like to think that if things had gone horribly wrong the other way around and we had to come to you to consider a higher fee you would be of a similar mindset to us and would have given it fair consideration. To be honest, while we could have justified the agreed fee the fee charged is a good recovery for the time undertaken and we did not need to incur any third-party research costs.'

There was a long period of silence then the Managing Director asked; 'Where are you now?' After explaining that she was on her way back to the office the Managing Director then asked if she was able to come back to his office for half an hour as he had a few other things he would like to discuss.

VALUE Creates Trust and Reciprocity

What transpired following that meeting was a long string of projects and assignments within the business units themselves that generated several hundred thousand dollars of fees over the years that followed.

CHAPTER 11

The Digital World

CHAPTER 11

The Digital World

Over the last ten years the world has witnessed a staggering technological transformation.

While changing every aspect of our lives this technological revolution has also impacted the application of the VALUE Encounter Methodology.

Nowhere has this been more evident than in the accounting profession where the VALUE Encounter Methodology was first applied to existing clients and networks.

While the range and spectrum of businesses deploying the VALUE Encounter Methodology in their business development activities has increased over the years, the approach was not been widely adopted by accounting firms.

Given that the application of the approach, to captive clients and networks, was first applied in an accounting practice the lack of uptake by the profession was particularly frustrating. In order to understand why this was the case an extensive review of the challenges currently facing the large number of mid-tier accounting firms, those with four or more partners, that were not considered second tier firms, was undertaken. This coincided with the establishment of the M-Institute, a not-for-profit organisation that was established to provide medium-sized businesses with a complementary first point of contact.

The M-Institute was founded in the United Kingdom to provide research into the drivers of medium-sized businesses, which are usually large employers, are growing rapidly and are attractive potential customers of the first- and second tier accounting firms.

Medium-size businesses are also critically important clients of mid-tier Accounting firms and the loss of even one could have a major impact on the average third or fourth tier firm.

What the review uncovered was the accounting profession's preoccupation with providing 'Advisory Services' to their clients. The profession was revealed to be increasingly concerned with the retention of their fee base which was identified on three fronts.

ONE
Larger Accounting firms, with a multitude of service offerings, were actively identifying and targeting growing medium-sized businesses as future business. These firms have considerable resources and extensive government connections, and are able to connect into medium-sized businesses on a number of fronts.

TWO
The large number of businesses that are owned by the aging baby boomer generation were increasingly engaging with larger firms that have Mergers & Acquisition expertise on the back of unsolicited approaches in relation to the sale of their business.

The emerging baby boomer wave of owners that are likely to want to sell their business over the next five to ten years; are commonly referred to as prospective succession planning clients by a wide range of professional services providers.

These businesses are also vulnerable to unsolicited offers and approaches by a large number of 'Advisors' which often commence with unrealistic expectations in much the same way as real estate agents inflate values of properties to obtain listings, then gradually bring the sellers back to the market.

THREE
The emergence of cloud-based accounting software that has rapidly improved the in-house administrative accounting productivity of smaller businesses, and potentially exposing the value proposition of their accounting firm's compliance fees, which are the core recurring income streams of the vast majority of third and fourth tier accounting firms.

There is no better example than Xero, the cloud-based accounting software that has provided the smaller end of the business market with cost effective, easy to use accounting software.

Not only has Xero empowered smaller businesses, it has also extensively marketed its software through accounting firms as being a major contributor to productivity improvements. It then went on to provide those firms that promote Xero to their client base, with accounting practice management software that streamlines seamlessly with their clients' accounting software.

Furthermore, they enabled a multitude of developers to connect to their software through an open API. These developers supply a variety of seamlessly integrated packages that extend into a wide variety of additional functionalities such as job tracking, job costing, enterprise planning, and forecasting.

The addition of these packages extends the use of the Xero accounting platform into those smaller businesses that are embracing technology and are more likely to be growing.

The review highlighted that these three areas of vulnerability are being extensively promoted within the profession as the primary reason why accounting firms, particularly third and fourth tier firms, should be embracing 'Advisory Services'.

On face value these are all very valid justifications but the next logical question is what do they mean by Advisory Services?

What Are Advisory Services?

nem provides Consultancy Services to businesses.

nem does not provide taxation, accounting, financial, regulatory or statutory advice or services. These are typically provided, with varying levels of sophistication and specialisation, by accounting firms.

Typically, accounting firms do not provide clients with Consultancy Services.

For some reason, however, the services provided by the accounting profession, and the services provided by consultants, have been bundled conveniently together as 'Advisory Services'.

We would contend that accounting firms provide clients with 'Value Added Services'. Services that complement their core taxation and compliance expertise.

Furthermore, the research undertaken showed that the vast majority of marketing to the accounting profession in relation to their necessity to move into Advisory Services is being undertaken by software suppliers to the accounting profession.

Those suppliers are predominantly cloud-based software and systems integration suppliers. Their software varies significantly, but as a general rule their products import client information from platforms like Xero, MYOB and Reckon and provide forecasting and varying analytical frameworks.

These outputs are being positioned as Advisory Services when they are in fact Value Added Services that complement core taxation and compliance services, and there are a multitude of Value Added Services that accounting firms can logically and seamlessly provide their clients.

Furthermore, the review highlighted that those firms that offer a complimentary range of Value Added Services have higher client retention rates and higher average fee profiles, and that there are a very large range of complimentary Value Added Services that can be provided.

What Are Value Added Services?

Only the top tier firms, and a handful of smaller firms offer genuine Advisory Services.

What has emerged over recent years, through the technological advancement of cloud solutions and integration is the emergence of a variety of products that assist the profession to provide Value Added Services.

These are being marketed as Advisory Services – they are not. They are products and tools that have the ability to migrate existing clients to a firm's Value Added Services.

The campaign to move to Advisory is justified on the threat of automation, the loss of compliance and the downward pressure this creates on standard taxation and compliance services. But the label of Advisory Services in most cases is incorrect and misleading.

The following are the identified hierarchy of typical Value Added Services that the accounting profession can provided.

Hierarchy of Value Added Services

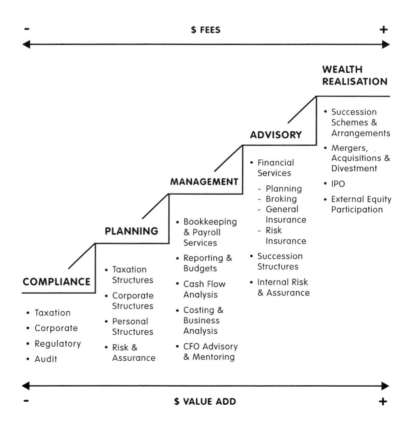

The critical decision for second and third tier accounting firms is to decide which Value Added Services it is going to provide AND then to ensure they are core competencies that are capable of being delivered effectively and efficiently.

The more Value Added Services provided to clients, the more sophisticated their structures are, and the more that they can rely on their accountants for the whole of life cycle of services, the more resilient the relationship will be, the more secure the client relationship and ownership transition, and the higher the fee base and profitability of the firm.

Third and fourth tier firms that embrace the necessity to provide competent, and in some areas highly specialised, Value Added Services do not find their fees under pressure and their clients are not at risk.

Clients and Fees Are Not at Risk

Progressive and competent accounting firms are wonderful businesses. They have loyal customers, with high levels of tax and compliance dependency, recurring revenue streams and the opportunity to build a suite of highly valuable Value Added Services, valuable to their clients and valuable to the firm.

Technology platforms and the products they provide need to be embraced as a Value Added delivery piece, not as a conversation piece.

Nothing can take over the human interaction, technology just enables this to happen more effectively and more efficiently than traditional VALUE Encounter interactions are!

Why Technology Remains Critical

The research undertaken by the M-Institute identified the six major barriers, obstacles and frustrations that owners of growing businesses face as they strive to grow and succeed in an ever changing economic and industrial landscape.

Unsurprisingly, their most precious resource is **TIME**. You cannot get your time back. Accounting firms need to be efficient, connect efficiently with clients and not waste their time and the time of their clients, determining what is important to clients.

As a result, most progressive firms can undertake very efficient low-touch digital campaigns that mimic Value Encounters with their Cats and Kittens, and can be very effective in identifying areas of interest across their entire client base. The key to those campaigns is the relevance of the messaging and the quality of the content that will follow.

The research of the M-Institute provides some valuable insights into what clients, and the partners within accounting firms, may be interested in.

While **TIME** featured as the most precious resource there were five other equally relevant challenges facing growing private businesses. In no particular order the other five are identified as follows:

1. Digital Technology

Digital technology rates highly as a barrier, not because it is necessarily seen as a threat, but more because business owners feel they need to embrace it, they just don't know how to do so.

Digital technology covers a wide range of disciplines and activities across many areas of business. This can include marketing, sales generation, infield services, mobile solutions, electronic integration in all areas of traditionally paper-based processes and systems. Digital technology has far reaching implications for every business operating in every conceivable market.

Digital technology has the ability to empower even very small businesses by providing affordable, robust and, in many cases, customised integrated platforms that utilise the security of hosted infrastructure and the agility and connectivity of cloud based mobile and hand-held solutions.

Those clients that are embracing technology expect their traditional service providers, including their accountants, to do the same when interacting with them, whether that be newsletters, correspondence or standard reporting.

Many accounting firms also believe that they need to embrace digital technology when marketing the firm's products and services and while this is fundamentally true, marketing outside their ecosystem and client networks is generally a waste of time.

Sending content digitally to people you do not know is just like cold calling, just quicker, easier to undertake but with very limited return on the investment.

What **nem** has perfected is the use of digital campaigns that mimic **VALUE** Calls with Cats and Kittens. These campaigns comprise personalised emails from each partner that encompass messaging that will resonate with business owners. As the recipient navigates their way through the introduction the platform monitors areas of interest and prepares to send varying levels of content on those areas that can be further analysed as opened.

Digitally, the areas and extent of client interest, on an individual basis is compiled with a call to action option for clients to request contact, or compiled and reported for the partner to initiate contact around known subject matters of interest.

2. Cash Flow

Cash flow, or lack of it, is the most common concern keeping business owners awake at night and as highlighted by the M-Institute is one of the most misunderstood areas of most businesses. 'Misunderstood' is not a lack of appreciation of the immediate cash flow issues of the business, it is a lack of understanding of the drivers and dynamics of cash flow.

Cash flow can often be put under enormous strain by growth. In fact, rapid growth can cause severe cash flow problems. As an example, large incremental sales of products or services with a 50% gross margin can create a cash crisis.

If the products or services need to be paid for in a cycle that is less than half of the collection, or sales cycle, then cash flow will be negative until the customer pays.

Add to this the complexity of multiple supplier inputs, expense cycles, accruing liabilities, movements in fixed costs and the accurate forecasting of immediate and future cash flow requirements of the business can become extremely difficult.

This lack of visibility is the most common cause of anxiety for business owners, followed closely by people-related issues.

At some point a business must take its management reporting to the next level. That means developing or accessing capability around the dynamics of the three-way cash flow matrix that affects cash flow – accounting for, reporting and forecasting profitability, working capital and balance sheet variations.

This is a prime Value Added Service platform for accounting firms.

3. Sale of the Business

Wide and varied research suggests that 70% of small to medium-sized business owners will be looking to exit their businesses over the next ten to fifteen years. Unlike the majority of smaller businesses, most profitable, medium-sized businesses are capable of attracting buyers[1].

The most critical objective is for the business to be prepared before the process commences, so the best possible outcomes can be achieved.

The accounting profession, more than any other service or product provider, has a unique capability of identifying the objectives, time lines and success of their client's journey.

---

[1] Source: There's a Perfect Storm Approaching for Existing Business Owners by Gary Ampulski, Midwest Genesis April 8, 2015

For the past two decades this opportunity has been referred to as 'succession planning'. This term is widely applied by a vast range of service and product providers. Accountants, lawyers, financial planners and bankers to name a few.

Unfortunately, the term 'succession planning' is despised by the target market. Research by **nem** has shown conclusively that the introduction of the subject to the vast majority of business owners is insulting.

The average sixty-five-year-old owner of a successful private business does not appreciate having the term raised to their face by a forty-year-old energetic professional. They see the term 'succession planning' as code for 'When are you retiring you old bugger?'

Digital marketing campaigns can be very effective in teasing out how progressed clients are in their thinking towards the sale of their business, and like **VALUE** Encounters this can be far more effectively determined positioning the **VALUE** of their business as the messaging.

We **VALUE** your business program, where is the **VALUE** of your business, where is the future **VALUE** of your business are all unobtrusive messages that can tease out interest and lead to next step traditional **VALUE** Encounters.

4. Sales Growth

Sales growth is the most common objective of businesses that are wanting to increase profitability. Many owners of businesses that fall into this category are constantly looking for quick fixes and silver bullets and this makes them vulnerable to slick consultants, sales gimmicks and manipulative tactics that often do not work.

Accounting firms are not immune either and are often at a loss to grow their fee base, let alone help their clients to navigate their way through the challenges that they face.

As we have seen through the application of the **VALUE** Encounter Methodology, the most efficient, cost effective and rapid way of achieving sales growth is to focus on the existing products and services that are sold to existing customers in existing markets.

As we saw with **cama**™, the key is to know which products or services have the greatest competitive advantage and then identifying the most attractive markets in which to position them.

And like most accounting firms, existing clients and customers provide significant organic growth and referral opportunities but this requires an intimate knowledge of every aspect of existing sales process.

Making small, incremental improvements to a number of aspects of the entire sales cycle and service or product offering can have a major impact on revenue, and more importantly, profitability.

There are of course a number of other methods to achieve increased sales, like acquiring competitors, launching into new markets or selling new products or services to existing customers.

These methods, however, usually require additional funds to finance them, as costs are usually required to be incurred before sales, and this is particularly relevant with acquisitions or the introduction of completely new products or services.

5. Assistance

One of the accelerators of successful businesses is reliance on assistance from third parties at various times and across a wide range of areas. Assistance is usually required at various stages of the growth cycle, on a project by project basis until the business can upskill internally or can afford to bring on their own resources.

To quote *The Breakthrough Company* by Keith R. McFarland:

> Third party providers are like scaffolding. They help to support the growth of the business, like scaffolding does when constructing a building. Once the business achieves its objectives the scaffolding (or assistance) is no longer required.

The first issue that all business owners need to overcome when obtaining third party assistance is the issue of who they trust to communicate with.

In most circumstances business owners do not openly discuss their issues and more likely to maintain a façade of success with many of the people with whom they interact.

The establishment of the M-Institute as a genuine not-for-profit organisation, with transparent sponsors, is one attempt to overcome this barrier.

And surprisingly, the vast majority of business owners do not have a trusted party with whom they can raise issues, concerns and frustrations; let alone their immediate to short term objectives.

What continues to confound **nem** is the lack of awareness by a very large number of business owners (and that includes partners of accounting firms) of how their existing ecosystem of customers, clients, suppliers already trust them and their businesses.

The VALUE Encounter Methodology can unlock the potential that already exists by unlocking the biases, and leveraging off the relationships and trust that already exists.

As technology changes the application of knowledge, and artificial intelligence is being applied across a wider and wider spectrum of industries, the one element that cannot be replaced but is highly valued is trust.

Customer Experience is Based on Trust

Client satisfaction, or the 'Customer Experience' is a critical factor and this transcends into 'Value Added' relationships which is the heart of the Value Encounter Methodology.

When there is trust the introduction of a party that is outside the standard supplier and customer relationship is a powerful valued-added activity.

It has the ability to genuinely add value, provided the introduction is respected, will strengthen the existing relationship, create reciprocity and create the foundation for continual referrals.

CHAPTER 12

Life's Business Journey

CHAPTER 12

Life's Business Journey

Business life commences in our youth. Whether in the industrialised past where children were exploited in the coal mines and factories, or the innocent desire for financial independence as was the case in my childhood, we start to engage commercially with people from a very early age.

My desire for real financial independence started with a burning desire to buy a brand new bike. Having received a second-hand bike from my father on my eighth birthday, a *new* bike became increasingly important to me. I wasn't encouraged to begin my financial independence: I had to convince my parents, who reluctantly agreed (at least my mother did) to allow me to start selling newspapers at the age of eight.

The paper I sold was *The Herald*, which produced several editions throughout the day. The only reason that selling papers was viable was the price. With the introduction of decimal currency, the threepence it cost to buy a paper converted to three cents, and this almost always resulted in a two cent tip, particularly when the buyer's car was stopped in a No Standing area and I hunted for change for an uncomfortable period of time.

Unfortunately, these tips virtually disappeared when the paper price increased to five cents and all I was left with was half a cent for every paper sold. A good evening was thirty or forty papers in hail, rain or shine. The new bike wasn't getting any closer.

Determined, I then started morning and afternoon paper delivery rounds. This did not pay much better, but the money was constant and there were annual tips at Christmas that were usually substantial if I made sure the papers were always placed in a dry place and if I reminded the household that little Johnny wished the household a very Merry Christmas. I also learned that a little Easter card did well, and personalising the cards by adding householders' names from the account records made an enormous difference to the number of tips, particularly if I had said hello a number of times. I was learning quickly that developing **RELATIONSHIPS** generated good outcomes! The only downside to the paper rounds was the need to appear six days a week, no matter what, at the same time each morning and night.

Covering for others became a temporary money boost that created a relationship with Mr Skully, the newsagent owner. Mr Skully determined which paperboys sold at the two hotels in his area, on evenings and weekends. When he became confident that he could call on me at a moment's notice to fill in for other boys and that I would not take short cuts when doing double rounds, a relationship developed based on Mutual Respect.

I respected his authority and he respected my reliability and professionalism.

That relationship resulted in my being assigned from time to time to the hotel evening paper sales – not all the time, because Mr Skully did not play outright favourites, and used his authority wisely by sharing the rewards around. I did, however, get my fair share, and I was able to undertake the hotel sales after the afternoon paper round. The hotel sales nearly always resulted in good tips, especially on Friday and Saturday evenings.

Within two years I managed to buy my new bicycle. That was my first commercial outcome from a business relationship based on mutual respect. My life's journey of **VALUE** Encounters had begun – not that I understood what that meant at the time. It required another thirty years of experience for me to create the **VALUE** Encounter Methodology that is outlined in this book: a framework created to accelerate business development activities through effective engagement, relying on the cornerstone of productive interaction in our communities **RELATIONSHIPS**.

There is no disagreement from any seasoned business development professional, learning and development specialist, or successful entrepreneur that relationships are the key to sustainable and successful outcomes. None of these people, however, have ever been able to explain to me why this is the case or do so in a way that provides less experienced staff with a framework that allows them to operate as efficiently and effectively as they do. As you have learned, *Treat Your Customers Like Animals* provides the reasoning and framework from which varying levels of relationships can be identified, and within which interaction can be varied to ensure the highest possible level of engagement.

The internationally acclaimed practical research undertaken by Dr Ian Freeman applied the **VALUE** Encounter in the business banking sector, and in so doing proved it is truly unique and the world's first relationship framework application.

The following experiences during the journey of my business life helped to anchor this framework. No doubt many of you have had similar experiences and encounters, which have developed your own intuitive approaches to relationships. What makes the experiences I outline unique to me is the way in which they allowed me to see behind the **FAÇADE** and to recognise the underlying Needs and Wants of the people and organisations I interacted with.

The Start

We all start our commercial lives at different times and in different ways. Some of us work for businesses, some start as budding entrepreneurs. My earliest entrepreneurial experience was selling lollies out the front of our house to passers-by when I was six. Not that we lived on a particularly busy street. That was the first problem. Only neighbours actually bought a lolly, and they only bought it out of sympathy, and only if they couldn't avoid walking past. There was also the odd stranger who bought a few, because they felt sorry for us or (more likely) thought my little sister was cute. We ate all the profits, too!

My second entrepreneurial experience was selling wooden pencil cases, which I had learned to make at woodwork classes when I was ten. These were made to order, and orders came from friends and family in a flurry at first, then, dried up. Pencil cases were profitable for the few months it took to sell them to every adult family member and friend I had. The gravitation to family and friends became a common recurring objective of many of the entrepreneurs I came into contact over the years, including our new partners as they started to evaluate the usefulness of their networks to their new role.

Different Respect for Different People

There were, of course, a myriad of jobs as I outgrew the paperboy sales and paper rounds. My first was a butcher's shop assistant after school for two hours a night. Nothing enjoyable emerged from that job and the owner was not a particularly engaging person. I nearly became a vegetarian as a result of my experiences in that job not because of the carcasses, blood or what I saw going into sausages, but because of the lack of scruples of the owner.

One afternoon I wasn't feeling particularly well, but I was loyal, reliable and determined to work. One of my tasks was to remove the trays of produce from the refrigerated window every night and carry them to the cool room for storage until the morning. On this particular afternoon I was carrying a tray of tripe, the shop didn't sell too much tripe and there certainly weren't any regulars I knew of who bought it. As I carried the tripe into the cool room, it wobbled around. I felt queasy and queasier, and threw up all over it. I dropped the tray on the floor, where the tripe, already covered in vomit, became coated in sawdust. I became distraught, fearing it was the end of my job. The owner rushed towards me and pushed me out the back to the bathroom so I could make no more mess.

Feeling better the next day, I returned to the shop after school to carry out the same routine. Not much was said as I cleaned out the window, where the same piece of tripe sat in the tray. I didn't say a word.

It took quite a few days before the tripe was sold and some fresh tripe took its place. While the owner liked tripe, he took none of the tripe from that tray home, selling it to unsuspecting and unknown customers rather than throwing it out and replacing it with fresh produce.

This was the first time I realised that when there was no relationship between people like the butcher and his unknown customers, there was quite possibly no **RESPECT**! Perhaps even disrespect for the standards held by oneself.

Reliability of Friends of Friends

The next job that shaped my business life was working in the corner shop. I felt like a child in a candy shop, so to speak, when I started work there, surrounded by lollies, chocolates, ice cream and drinks, although I was in my mid-teens by this stage. The owners were really clever. They were very clear that I could eat what I wanted, when I wanted, provided all the jobs were done (and there were numerous tasks, from putting the empty bottles out the back to stocking the shelves to cleaning, cleaning and more cleaning). I didn't eat packaged products, and I never – and I mean never – ate or drank in front of customers.

The shop was always busy, people popping in and out constantly, so I had no chance to eat my fill. Then a few really quiet spells allowed me to go full bore. It only took a few big milk shakes and gorging on mixed lollies while on my feet for many hours to make the produce far less attractive than it had appeared at the outset of the job. The attractive **FAÇADE** of the perks soon gave way to monotony of the job and the long hours on my feet and I started to enjoy friends dropping in.

After a few months the business was sold and to my delight the new owners were lovely people who trusted me implicitly. They had not owned a business before and it soon became apparent that the early mornings and late nights, seven days a week, were a burden. Mr Bliss also held down a security officer's job, which meant shift work. Soon I found myself alone on weekends and during quiet periods. The original owners had never allowed staff to work on their own. I never **UNDERSTOOD** why, until a few of my friends starting hanging around. I would let them have a few lollies, like I did, and share my milkshakes occasionally, until I noticed that they started taking this for granted and expecting things.

It came to a head one Saturday afternoon when my best friend came in with a few of his friends, whom I knew but not well. They were a rough lot. Simon's mother worked and could not discourage him from seeing the sort of kids that other parents disapproved of. As they milled around the shop I got more and more anxious. Then one of his friends opened a packet of chips, which I duly asked him to pay for. He laughed, and another one picked up some chocolate; when the three of them had taken numerous items they left the shop.

I panicked and could not think clearly. My instinct was to chase them, but I couldn't leave the shop. A customer came in who knew me; he could see I was flustered and asked what had happened. I explained that some kids who were friends of my mate had just stolen some items. He told me to call the police. My mate screamed for them to come back or the police would be called. The customer ran out of the shop with him, which seemed to give the threat some real substance.

As this was unfolding the owner returned. I quickly briefed him and he was off like a rocket, and soon had the three rounded up. He had just come off shift and was armed – not that he drew his gun or anything, but let's say he had the group's measure. The unopened items were returned, and they paid for what they could and provided the owner with their names and details so he could get paid for the balance.

I never found out if the owner got paid but I certainly offered to have the money deducted from my pay, which he never did. I felt that I had breached his trust by letting such an indiscretion creep into my behaviour with **FRIENDS**. I never again allowed friends to hang around, and it put me off eating lollies, and drinking milkshakes as well for that matter, for a long time.

The First Business Referral

The next job, which had an impact on me was as a drive-thru bottle shop attendant at a busy local hotel. This was a great job. The hours suited my lifestyle, being mainly nights and weekends, and the hourly rates were exceptional. Not only was I now paid as an adult, but the hours I worked were always time and a half or double time with penalty loadings and allowances. I couldn't believe how good it was. The reason I knew about the job was because a good friend told me about his job and told me he would let me know when there was an opening. He **REFERRED** me to the right manager, and soon after that I started. This job enabled me to save enough money to buy my first car, an HR Holden that needed a lot of work.

It was a very busy job, particularly on Saturday nights. The hotel had a three-lane drive-thru, and during busy periods one of us would sit at the till and enter the orders as they were yelled out, confirming the amount by yelling it back, and having the denomination yelled back so the change could be given immediately when the money was handed over. The managers usually operated the till as they had a more thorough knowledge of the products and also because they didn't have to run around all night. The main bottle shop boss was pretty lazy but none of us blamed him. As a manager he worked crazy hours for not a lot of money. We were all students and were going to university, so we aspired to rise to well above hotel manager status; at least we did once we understood the industry.

One of our jobs was to cut down beer cartons. We cut them into half-dozen's for the beer chutes, as large bottles were the preferred packaged beer of the day. The chutes were in the cool room and slanted towards the doors, which were accessed from the drive-thru. I had to stand on two full cartons just to start the cut at the top, and as I cut I would scoop each half dozen in one arm and cradle them down to two other attendants, who would put them in the chutes or behind the chutes for later. One Saturday afternoon while I was cutting cartons, I cut my little finger pretty badly. One half-dozen slipped, and as I tried to catch them the bottles started to break and the glass sliced into my finger. Blood was everywhere, and the mess in the cool room was serious. A lot of the stacks needed to be taken down before the bottom levels became unstable because of the spilt beer. We were pretty good at it, though and the place was spick and span in no time, with only three breakages.

But my finger took the worst of it, and blood kept seeping through the bandage. This meant I was placed on the till which I could do quite well. The till was standing height on a wine stand, and sitting on a bar stool meant you could sit down (which is why the lazy manager liked it – in addition to monitoring our activity).

Strangers Represent Risks

There was regular foot traffic at the drive-thru as well as the cars, and I noticed an odd-looking fellow off to one side who seemed to be taking a long time to select a wine. When there was a quiet spell he moved closer, coming behind me. He pushed his coat into my side and told me he had a knife and would stick me if I didn't open the till and hand over the money.

I had been pretty relaxed during the quiet spell, balancing the bar stool on two legs. Now I panicked and turned to open the cash register, with my good hand of course, and lost my balance. I fell back onto the thief. He in turn fell back into the spirit shelves, knocking bottles everywhere and creating an enormous crash. He jumped up, grabbed a stash of money, and was gone before I could get to my feet. The manager saw him and gave chase; security was called and before the burglar could escape he had cornered himself in the car park. A rather dishevelled looking guy who you could not help to feel sorry for, surrendered to the police, who arrived in minutes.

He did indeed have a knife, quite a large one, which was found by police in front of the crowd that had gathered. He was subsequently charged and I went back to the police station to give a statement. Before giving the statement, the sergeant gave me a lecture for standing up to armed robbers but eventually he realised I had simply panicked and accidently knocked him over.

Needless to say, even though I did give a complete and honest account to the police I was considered a pretty brave fellow by my colleagues, the other bar staff and more importantly the manager and owners. The **FAÇADE** of bravery gave me instant acceptance, and notoriety followed this dramatic event. Offers from the waitress of drinks after work were graciously and humbly accepted.

Reputation Does Not Provide Security

This new-found status didn't save me from being retrenched a fortnight later. My friend Trevor, three other hard-working drive-thru attendants and I came to pick up our pay, to be told we were no longer needed. When I questioned this, I was told it was due to theft and a high level of stock losses. The hotel, and particularly the bottle shop, had tight stocktake procedures. Some random items were checked daily, sometimes more than once or twice a day; and bulk items were checked at least weekly.

Occasionally staff would be questioned about discrepancies, but we didn't see the terminations coming.

I **ASKED** the full-time manager why he thought it was me: where was the evidence, what shifts, which items, what patterns? My **OPEN** questions had him reeling, and rightfully so. Eventually he admitted he didn't know who it was but said the last time we were quizzed about beer losses, I had explained that another manager often removed several dozen bottles at a time from the bottle shop. I kept up with the **OPEN** questions and discovered his only justification for sacking me was that if I had not reported suspicious behaviour in the past I was likely to be dishonest in the future.

Keep Asking Questions

He said the losses were too big for one person to undertake themselves without other staff noticing, so there must have been collusion (now he was a lazy private investigator as well). His conclusion was since the five of us were friends we must have been in it together, which accounted for the large amounts stolen.

Most discrepancies were due to wrong items being keyed into the register, but even if this occurred the cash would nearly always gel with any overcharges picked up by the customers. I was relentless, now becoming more and more specific. Some losses were stock transfers not accounted for, but there were also odd items: a spirit, two or three wines, half a dozen crown lagers, etc. Still not understanding the connection, I kept going with the **OPEN** questions. Steal what? Was it packaged, spirits or wine? When was it detected? On how many occasions were there losses? In which areas were the losses located?

All he told me was it was mainly beer, and lots of it, over the past few weeks.

My questioning was to no avail. We were told that was it: the five of us were fired.

Listening Means You Care

I went home annoyed at first, and then disappointed as I started to absorb the implications for my future. They were accusing me of being no better than the thief two weeks earlier. I couldn't believe that in a fortnight I could be seen as an honest, brave employee and then as a thief. They had no witnesses or evidence.

Dad came home late that night and could tell something was wrong. When I went to bed he came in to see me. Now that I was eighteen, that didn't happen very often. When he asked if he could come in, sat on the end of my bed and was genuinely compassionate, I became even more upset, on the verge of crying. He **ASKED** a few **OPEN** questions and out it came. He sat and **LISTENED** without interruptions, and looked simply astonished.

Core Values Never Change

My dad, an accountant himself, worked for the State Electricity Commission and also undertook a wide range of voluntary roles, particularly in the education system, and ended up as the treasurer in most organisations because of his accounting background. This saw him administering funds and often handling fundraising cash contributions. Dad was as honest as they came, and he appeared to really understand the depth of my despair.

Communicating Facts Not Emotion

After first **LISTENING** and then **ASKING** a few pertinent questions, he told me not to worry and that he would look into the matter the next day. I had a restless night but went off to university as usual in the morning, then caught up with my friend, who was also fired and at a loss. He wasn't even told why (as I later found out was industry practice when theft was involved) so my understanding of the facts really shook him as well!

Dad came home unusually early that evening and sat me down in his office. On the way home from work he had arranged to meet the owner of the hotel, a very wealthy businessman. He was not the licensee: his senior resident manager was, with three managers reporting to him including the one who sacked me. Dad told me that the owner was going to personally look into the matter and contact me. I didn't give too much credence to this, but appreciated Dad going out of his way to look into the matter. But sure enough the next day while I was at university the owner rang my mother and wanted me to go and see him at 5 pm at the hotel, which I duly did, not knowing what to expect.

Understanding the Facts

The owner handed me a letter stating I was a gainfully employed bottle shop attendant of unquestionable honesty. He went on to explain that the young manager I had observed moving packaged beer on a number of occasions was in fact his brother's son (his nephew), whom he had reluctantly hired as a trainee manager. This was a mistake, as his brother now thought he had free rein through his son, and his son thought he had a right to anything he wanted. There had been a number of charges in the bar and bistro sent to the owner's private account, and his nephew often took items from the bottle shop on the account as well.

The large stock losses were the result of his nephew failing to record beer he had taken for a series of family events over recent weeks. He did not record them as transfers as he had in the past because there had been repercussions on the last dozen occasions. 'Better not to record them and then no one will know,' was his explanation. I was dumbfounded, but back at work at 6 pm together with my mate, who received a similar letter and phone call.

On reflection I was relieved that I had kept **ASKING** why, and did not **BLINDLY** accept the situation. I later learned that it was industry practice (an unspoken code) to never explain why a casual was fired for theft and to never give them a reference. So, the lazy manager at least had a conscience by admitting to the facts upon interrogation. These facts enabled the owner to review the circumstances properly, and find his own family member was at fault.

I was lucky that my father had **LISTENED** to every aspect of my recollection of events, and gave the owner enough information to look into the matter thoroughly.

Another Referral

Coinciding with my employment at the bottle shop, I started dating a girl whose older sister was in some of my classes at university. Their mother was the matron of a geriatric hospital that was near the hotel I worked at. My girlfriend worked there part-time as a nursing aide, and I often dropped in before or after my shifts at the hotel to meet her. It was not the most pleasant environment, but I often had to wait for her and got into the habit of chatting with a few of the residents (inmates, they used to be called). The majority were women in their late seventies to early nineties, and I got to know quite a few of them.

One of the reasons it wasn't pleasant was the style of food (always mushy stuff) and the smell, best described as stale urine, due to poor cleaning. It wasn't long before my comments inspired the matron (my girlfriend's mother) to offer me a cleaner's job. I thought it was a joke at first, but she offered Saturdays and Sundays as a casual from 8 am to 2 pm. Penalty rates again and it was a perfect fit with the hotel job.

So, I started cleaning. I used masses of disinfectant and cleaning fluids to freshen up the place, and always cleaned thoroughly under the beds and chairs. I chatted with the inmates as I went around, and received friendly banter back on a regular basis.

I soon had the routine mastered and enjoyed the conversations with the inmates even more than the cleaning! In fact, the more efficient I became the more time I had to chat, so I got to know a number of them very well. I got to know a lot about their families too: whom the inmates liked and who they didn't; their views on who really cared, and even their intended beneficiaries.

We Take People for Granted

It was quite funny when visitors arrived, often family members who hadn't visited for many months and sometimes a year. I knew more about them than they could possibly imagine. They treated me as the cleaner, the hired help, with total disregard as if I could not **LISTEN** to what they were saying. The **FAÇADE** that some relatives conveyed of caring about and missing their mother, grandmother or grandfather was quite sickening. These infrequent visitors always made for interesting banter the next day between the inmates and me! This was one of the least pleasant aspects of the job – witnessing the infrequent visits by family relatives who pretended they cared when their infrequency was testament to the contrary. It was particularly exasperating with those who lived locally and missed key dates like birthdays, Christmas and Easter.

After a few months I started to take the job for granted, and often didn't get to bed early enough to make a sprightly start on Sunday mornings. In fact, I was often hungover, which limited the extent of my banter with the inmates. Instead of carefully cleaning around the non-compos inmates' feet, I just slopped the mop around, often wetting their 'house regulation' fluffy slippers. To my surprise, one Sunday as I entered a ten-bed ward of non-compos inmates, one yelled out, 'Here comes Johnny with the mop.' To my surprise these immobile, non-communicative inmates all raised their feet in the air. From then I made this a deliberate ploy to see if the rest could react, and within a few months they all lifted their feet, could chat and knew who I was. The vast majority of nurses, over many years, had stopped talking to these patients because they appeared to be unable to talk – but they could in fact still **LISTEN**. I realised that we can't stop communicating with the people whom we interact with regularly without falling into a malaise and a miserable disposition.

I also quickly learned that people take others for granted (as visitors did to me, as a cleaner), talk as if the people they take for granted do not have ears and become **BLIND** to the facts. But everyone has ears, even non-compos patients, so we can never assume we are not being heard or **UNDERSTOOD** just because the desired response is not always given.

I retained my job at the hospital until I started my first full-time professional job with one of the top tier chartered accounting firms.

The Rules Change Once You are Trusted

Before the full-time role as a graduate with the accounting firm, I had one more job over a Christmas break as a process worker at a cheese-processing factory, which helped me understand business relationships.

A friend told me about the jobs over Christmas and the money was really good. I went for the interview and medical and was told I could start straight away as a trainee, if I passed.

As I went through the undignified medical I discovered I was colour blind. They asked me to say what number I saw, and I asked, 'What number?' That was the first card. It didn't get any better. I found out later that Dad was colour blind too, and I had inherited his genes. Red and green – just hopeless.

As I resigned myself to not starting, the examiner said that it was disappointing as I would be unable to operate a machine. I asked what she meant, and she explained that all machines from cutters to conveyers had a green start button and a red stop button. Because I was colour blind I would be limited to process lines and packing, never an operator. On that note I was handed a white uniform: pants and t-shirt, hair net and white beret. The trousers were too short and I looked a complete idiot. After five minutes looking in the mirror, I knew I couldn't go through with it. I walked out of the changing room and through a door (there were three or four to choose from) into the canteen, and could not believe my eyes. There must have been 500 workers who looked just like me! I was not that odd after all.

So, thinking about the pay, I made a reverse entry back to the changing room and the medical section, where I was ushered into a room with several other recruits and shown an industry video. We were then assigned to production teams of eight people: two new temporary full-timers and six permanents. The other temporary full-timer on the line was the priest of a small Christian parish. He was trying to bolster his income, which was primarily from wedding and christening fees.

What an eye-opener that job was. I spent the first few days on the Swiss cheese line. There were two Swiss cheese lines operating ten to twelve hours a day, every working day. I was told they supplied the whole of Australia.

The job was boring. It wasn't too long before I was figuring out more efficient ways to perform each task and getting to know the permanent staff. The permanents were down-to-earth, hard-working people who did what they were shown without too much inventiveness. My techniques and suggestions soon had me operating the cutting machines, and our group soon had the highest yield and efficiency of the two lines.

Small bonuses accrued to the permanents as a result, but I was not too popular as I never moved from that role. I wasn't even supposed to be operating the machine, a fact that my supervisor assured me was not an issue.

As he explained, I was accepted onto the line and I could clearly distinguish the red stop and green start buttons on the machine, so no problem.

I realised that it didn't really matter what the entry requirements were once you were in. The game changed entirely when you entered their environment – you were judged on your merits. Provided you met the entry requirements, the actual conditions, procedures and protocols you carried out could be quite different to those that were used to determine your eligibility.

I soon found myself on the 'cheese powder room' roster. No one liked the cheese powder processing line. I was told that after a week on that line I would be finding cheese in places I didn't know existed. It was a pretty aggressive machine, according to the room supervisor, who briefed me and provided protective gear. I quickly explained that being colour blind I would be unable to operate the machine, according to the medical health and safety staff. He made a call and I was back on the Swiss cheese line, swapped with the priest. Despite his Christian values he was never as pleasant after that, despite my attempts to chat with him as I had previously done over breaks and lunch intervals. I realised I had lost his **RESPECT** and I could not get it back no matter how hard I tried.

Ask If You Do Not Understand

The graduate role with a large international chartered accounting firm was my first real professional job. I was offered a graduate auditor position after a series of campus interviews with all the major accounting firms. I had two offers and decided, on advice from my father, to choose the firm that had an excellent reputation for training graduates.

Knowing that this was a serious career, I resigned from all my casual jobs, purchased two suits and a new car with a personal loan, courtesy of my father, and found myself clean shaven, nicely groomed and ready to head off for my first day at work. Dad left late that day to see me off, and offered a few words of advice as I was about to walk out the door.

In the past, Dad had given me a great deal of advice, which I had never acted upon, but this time I **LISTENED** intently. Perhaps it was the fact that I was entering a world he knew better than me. He told me, 'Son, you are going to meet a lot of clever and capable people at the firm. They will be explaining and showing you what to do for quite a while, so please just promise me one thing: if for any reason you do not **UNDERSTAND** what they are asking you to do, make sure you **ASK** straight away. Try not to feel embarrassed because you do not understand; just ask politely until you do.'

He explained that if I didn't ask I would feel compelled later on to bluff that I did, in fact, understand, and the person doing the explaining would assume I was on top of things. He went on to say that if I was going to take this first job seriously I had to understand what I was doing at the start of each new area, as any gap in knowledge would widen as I was introduced to more and more businesses and processes.

The first week was training week, and was quite straightforward. There were about twenty of us in my intake for audit, and on the last day we were introduced to the audit of the bank reconciliation. This was supported by a small audit manual that recorded each procedure step by step. This was the first time I asked 'why?' in relation to the reverse nature of the checking process. The trainer referred me back to the manual, but I still didn't get it. It made no sense to me how it was stepped out, so I asked again, only to referred to the manual again. Twice was enough, I was too embarrassed to ask again in front of my colleagues as everyone else seemed to understand.

When I came home I asked Dad, who explained that the reverse check ensured that you captured book entries purporting to be bank statement entries, as opposed to checking if the bank statement entries had been recorded correctly in the books. A two-way check, so to speak. The bigger the bank account the more random the checks were, but they were there to ensure both records accurately reflected cash movements.

After the first week I was assigned to a management group and started working on clients and at client premises. Most tasks consisted of writing work programs from the previous year's files, checking field sizes, and following the same audit programs from the year before. This was when my questions really started to get some interesting responses. To my surprise many supervisors, assistant managers and managers would become impatient and not answer my questions about some of the tasks they were asking me to do. I don't mean the simple steps themselves; I mean the logic behind each step.

I remember one client file in relation to auditing the circulation data for a newspaper. It involved checking the newspaper circulation count on site at random intervals. The prescribed paper step was to record and validate the counter at the end of the press, which without going there made perfect sense. On site, however, it was clear that the counter included tallies of discarded papers and spoilage as well as proper papers. Dispatch recorded *all* bundles and quantities delivered, and by definition these were the papers put into the distribution system – but this was not recorded. If this was the case, and I really was not 100% sure, the circulation figure reported on the certificate was overstated by approximately 15%.

I recorded both counts by adding another three steps to the audit procedure, and when I was in the office the next day I asked the manager why the press counter was recorded but not the dispatch counter. He looked at me strangely and gave me an explanation that I could not understand, so I asked him again, politely of course. He couldn't explain why. He told me to complete the certificates as they were always done, and was very insistent. I did as I was told but left a detailed note on the file saying that I believed the dispatch counter should be the primary source for circulation verification.

What I didn't know at the time was that files were randomly reviewed by partners from an internal quality and assurance section and due to the length of the audit this client file was extensively reviewed. As a consequence, my file note was read. At some point over the last seven or eight years someone had recorded the wrong count source and it had simply been replicated ever since. The circulation figures were the driver of advertising revenue and verified reach, so the implications were very serious.

Please do not misunderstand. The firm was made up of a very intelligent and capable group of professionals. To some extent it was almost intimidating for me but I learned from this and many other experiences that I could not take all explanations and representations from my colleagues at face value. It was critical to **ASK** why, before reaching conclusions for myself.

Understanding is the First Step to Learning

Because I understood the tasks I was undertaking as I progressed up the ranks of the firm, I could explain tasks and technical matters to others very well; it was not long before I had graduates reporting to me. This was followed by a succession of under-performing graduates and supervisors for whom I was the last hope. If I couldn't train them, then they needed to look at options other than audit in the firm.

The professional year came along, and to my great surprise on passing I was asked if I would like to work in staff training in addition to my audit role. This was a genuine honour, and despite my dislike of public speaking I accepted the role, which was for two years, and undertook 'train the trainer' training.

I also held down some key audit commitments with major companies, and after leaving staff training started to build my client portfolio. Although only a senior, I managed portfolios as if I was an assistant manager, and as a result I worked primarily for senior managers who were vying for partnership. What I saw developing was an expectation that these managers would drive new business. This really interested me, because new business as an auditor meant new clients, and new audits were often tendered by clients or were presented to us because of overseas affiliations.

The prospect of bringing in new client activity directly from one's own business development activities was daunting. Without any guidance or assistance from the firm (which I was aware of due to my involvement in the national staff training program), most managers tried to be speakers at a wide range of forums and seemed to me to attend events endlessly, often after hours and on weekends. Being a rather introverted person, I did not find this kind of pressure at all appealing.

Another Referral

As I was seriously contemplating the next step to manager and then (hopefully) partner, I was approached by an audit client, a printer of business forms, to accept a senior finance role reporting to the expatriate Chief Financial Officer (CFO). The CFO had a management and commercial background and was not familiar or confident with public company financial reporting and protocols. This meant my role would carry a breadth of responsibility that was not normally required at my level, and was a critical support for the CFO, particularly in relation to the statutory financial reporting requirements of the company.

The responsibility was significant, as was the package I managed to negotiate, which gave me the confidence and financial capacity to buy a home with my fiancée soon after I commenced with the company.

Some Friends Come from Business

The CFO was an expatriate who moved to Australia with his family. His wife was a delightful person and it was not long before the assistance I provided in helping them to settle in outside work hours resulted in a genuine friendship.

The CFO came from what I learned was a stable and long held middle management role within the North American parent company. He demanded a level of management reporting that staggered me and I learned a lot about the importance of accurate and timely operational accounting and reporting from him. I soon was assembling a strong management accounting team to upgrade the systems and the reporting.

While he backed me, supported the development of my department and had very strong operational capability, his strategic horizon was limited and his willingness to back a young group of aspiring executives was out of step with the traditional promotional path he had experienced. The Board also made a series of poor strategic acquisition decisions, which evolved to limit my advancement opportunities, in terms of wider experience and financial remuneration. As a result, I left after a few years to take up a role with a private dyeing and finishing company operating in the besieged textile industry.

We All Have Knowledge

If I thought I knew a bit, this was the real eye opener: a 100-year-old family business staffed by veterans who marched to the drum of a demanding third-generation owner. The first thing I learned was that cash was king. Despite widespread due diligence, the business was barely solvent when I joined, and required immediate refinancing. I found out later that this was why they were looking for a new CFO: the financiers had lost confidence in the financial management of the business.

The reporting was poor and the staff were, in my immediate assessment, incapable of following my lead, so I quickly started to plan for new blood. Out with the old and in with the dynamic new as I had done at the business forms business quite successfully. But with an uncertain future before the company it was not right to bring in new staff on the promise of a great career path, particularly when enticing them away from secure employment. So I was stuck with the old guard, which became a really empowering process.

Learning to Respect Others

As cash dried up, efficiencies needed to be extracted and costs reduced. I found that the experienced staff could provide all the secrets and delve into the **UNKNOWN** areas of the business (to me) where there was waste, who the really knowledgeable operators were, which customers could be relied upon and which ones could not. I just had to obtain their confidence, show genuine respect and **ASK** the right questions.

The depth of these seemingly incapable people's knowledge was unbelievable, and their loyalty unquestionable. When things got really tough they did what they were asked and were incredibly important in maintaining a viable business during an extremely volatile and uncertain period.

Interest rates on the main financing facility were 24% and a recession appeared to be looming. The primary banker supported the business (through which a very strong relationship developed) with the local business bank manager. We were not friends, but each had strong

MUTUAL RESPECT for the other. I provided the facts and forecasts, and he supported the business both within his authority and beyond it, by influencing others in the bank.

Contacts Cannot Always be Trusted

Not long after refinancing the business with the primary bankers, the finance company with whom the business factored its debts, sent in investigating accountants to assess its position. During this uncertain time I was approached by an executive search firm, to go back to the business forms company as CFO, as the CFO I had worked for was returning home.

A new CEO, another North American expatriate, interviewed me but was unable to answer my questions about the future of the company. This confirmed my belief that the company was no closer to a clear strategic direction and remained terrified of the change to a paperless office. I decided to stick with the fabric business and declined the job offer. The new CEO could not believe my decision. I gave two reasons to the search firm: a lack of strategic focus, and that my departure from my current employer could hasten its demise.

The search firm conveyed these to the new CEO who interviewed me, and before I knew it the third-generation owner had me out to coffee one morning, pleading for me to stay. When I asked him what he was carrying on about he said the CEO of my last employer had telephoned him and asked him why he was holding me ransom to the success or otherwise of the business. He believed the job offer was still in play so he was trying to keep me, offering ridiculous money and incentives.

I assured him I wasn't going anywhere, and was really unimpressed that the CEO had breached the confidentiality of the search firm's approach to me and of our discussions.

The search firm had also breached a confidential matter. One of the reasons I left the business in the first place was the CFO's lack of support and vision, so a few days later I had an angry CFO on the phone, asking if this was correct. His attitude confirmed my decision. My father was devastated that I didn't take the job but didn't raise the subject ever again.

We All Have an Agenda

The dyeing and finishing company survived the independent review by the insolvency firm appointed by the factoring company, which was a great relief. This review produced another interesting development. The manager who was undertaking the review saw the business as insolvent and wanted his firm to be appointed administrator. The owner did not agree, and neither did I. Despite the obvious difficulties facing the textile industry the owner had done one thing that was extremely clever: he positioned the dye house as a critical quality-endorsed hub of the Australian knitted fabric industry. This meant that all Australian clothing manufacturers that supplied a top tier retailer needed to buy his quality endorsed fabrics.

This saw the business invest in knitting machinery and fabrics in addition to their traditional commission dyeing business. Dyeing and finishing fabrics was a capital-intensive business with extensive overheads and capacity. The dye houses were like the hub of a wheel to the wider textile industry. Without a dye house, fabric wholesalers and manufacturers could not supply retailers. The dye house was also critical to two elements of the end quality of the garment: the quality of the dyeing controlled the colourfastness (how much the dye would run when washed); and the finishing quality controlled the shrinkage (how much the garment would shrink when washed). Knowing this, the owner devised a process that guaranteed colourfastness and non-shrinkage, and introduced the concept to the likes of Target. Target not only specified that all local garments needed to meet this standard, but also advertised that their garments were guaranteed not to shrink or run.

What made this strategy even cleverer was that no other local dye house had the sophisticated equipment to ensure appropriate tolerances could be achieved without massive increases in operating costs. This was a genuine competitive advantage, although the business was only starting to deploy it when the financial troubles commenced. This competitive advantage did not translate to price as the industry was ruthlessly competitive, but it did result in increasing volumes. The new strategy required enormous levels of working capital and cash (hence the use of factoring) to finance the purchase of yarns and their knitting into fabrics.

As volumes increased, so did profitability despite rock bottom prices. As the volumes increased the fixed costs remained flat and despite the industry and overall volumes having contracted to historically low levels the business was capable of performing exceptionally well.

But the forecasts of the company's profitability were not believed to be accurate by the investigating accountant who saw them as too ambitious for an industry under siege. I was twenty-nine, with a significant mortgage. The investigating accountant started to threaten my professional future in an effort to convince me that I should declare the business insolvent and unable to trade out of its difficulties. This was really nasty stuff: 'As the CFO you can be held personally liable if the business is to fail.' These threats went as far as phone calls to my wife, informing her of the same opinions.

The grief and concern this person caused was significant. This was the first time I sought the professional advice of an outsider, an experienced accountant and insolvency practitioner who understood the business and was supportive.

Some Relationships are Timeless

That person was a partner from the firm that audited the company. His advice gave me peace of mind and provided a path to deal with the investigating accountant and we have remained in touch ever since. I made a formal report of his conduct to the Institute of Chartered Accountants, and asked that it be noted on the record but not acted upon until the future of the business was known. A formal statement went on file and gave me some piece of mind.

The business battled on for the next two years but the recession of the early 1990s took its toll. A series of bad debts saw the factoring company start to call in its loans. They were a ruthless organisation, and rather than act and face the potential legal consequences they slowly reduced the advances on invoices purchased. This meant they were reducing their loans but owned the entire debtors' book as collateral. By the time we were aware of their intent, the business was struggling to pay wages.

When we eventually stopped forwarding them the invoices (or selling the invoices to them) and negotiated our own payment arrangements (which was perfectly legal), they appointed receivers. That was the end of the business, my job and the jobs of 250 people.

The receivers were not the ones that undertook the investigation two years earlier, so after much deliberation I decided not to proceed with an official complaint against the manager.

Relatives are Very Different

While all this was transpiring in the middle of a significant recession, mortgage interest rates were in the high teens, my job was uncertain and I had a significant mortgage, my little sister was charged with drink driving. This devastated my parents, who were now retired and living a relatively quiet life.

It was uncharacteristic of her. I **ASKED** a series of questions and eventually got to the bottom of what happened. It became apparent that the charges were not an accurate portrayal of events. She had had an accident on the way to a nightclub in a quiet industrial area of the inner-city suburb: she drove up a gutter and into a cyclone fence, rendering the car immobile. With no other cars involved, no one hurt and her car not drivable, her friends convinced her not to call for assistance at such a late hour but simply to leave the car and deal with it the next day. They caught a taxi to the nightclub where my little sister had a few drinks. Upset by the accident she eventually left and caught a taxi back to the scene and called the RACV, who called a tow truck, who advised the police. The police asked her to undertake a breathalyser. She exceeded the limit and was charged with exceeding the legal blood alcohol level.

Knowing the facts, I asked my neighbour, a local solicitor, to look into the matter to see if she had a defence. To our surprise she did, provided she could prove the accident occurred at least three hours before she was charged, which on the evidence of her friends, she could. A defence was agreed and a barrister was to be briefed.

The only reason she had a defence, despite the fact that she did not exceed the legal limit at the time of the accident, was because the police had mistakenly charged her under an old section of the legislation. New legislation had been introduced six months earlier that removed the three-hour restriction. This was to prevent drivers under the influence from fleeing the scene and avoiding the police for at least three hours. The new section, however, was an extended subsection of the old subsection, and the police officer had recorded the old section by mistake on her summons. This meant a barrister could get the charge dismissed, but my sister had to leave the court before the prosecutors twigged, as they could object to the decision as long as she was still on the premises. My neighbour suggested we appoint an inexperienced barrister so as not to alert the prosecution that there was a genuine defence.

Only one problem: she had no money. Against my wife's advice I agreed to fund her defence on the agreement she would repay me when she could. I was convinced it was worth the punt for the sake of my little sister's reputation and the concern of my aging parents. I paid the $3000, the court date arrived, and she was found not guilty. Done deal - not guilty, no ability to appeal, no conviction, no fine and no stigma.

I rang Mum, who cried with joy. Then I asked my sister where she was going as she wandered down the street with her friends. 'I am off to celebrate, of course.'

'This is fantastic; you can now repay the cost.'

She replied, 'I've got no money, what are you talking about?'

'That was the deal, and now you don't even have to pay a fine.'

She went into a huff and ran off with her friends. That experience was upsetting at the time, and while it did not affect my genuine love of my little sister, it did highlight once again that family members treat their **RELATIONSHIPS** with one another far differently than they do with their wider networks. While there might be love and kindness there is often a lack of a conscious effort to maintain **MUTUAL RESPECT** and the situations of one or more parties can be quite effortlessly taken for granted.

I now understood why the hotel owner reluctantly employed a family member as a manager so many years ago.

First Impressions Count

My view was that an adequate job, rather than the perfect job, was probably more important, and accordingly I was prepared to accept a job beneath my capability in order to get a start in an organisation.

This is when I met a recruiter who immediately recognised me as a perfect candidate for a role at an Australian multinational paper and packaging company. I was clearly overqualified, but he knew I was a good fit. The old cheese processor experience had taught me that entry requirements didn't restrict opportunities once you were on the inside, so I accepted a role for half the money I was accustomed to, and joined the folding carton arm of a large company. The job required me to drive about as long as you could manage without leaving metropolitan Melbourne.

As I had thought, once in the head office accounts role I soon was involved commercially across the entire business and got involved in tenders and customer negotiations. I had handled all levels of commercial negotiation at the dyeing and finishing company and quickly introduced commercial responses to tenders that, based on the research around each individual customer's **NEEDS**, meant they would be unable to be dismissed on face value. Every submission gave the customers what they **WANTED** while requiring them to do things that we **NEEDED** to ensure they obtained the prices, quality and service they demanded.

Networking is Easy When the Topics Are of Interest

While I was still relatively unknown within the group, the board of the parent company held one of their revolving monthly board meetings at the head office of the subsidiary I worked in. The facility had an enormous boardroom that enabled catering and could seat thirty-odd people in formal lunch format. The board meeting ran for the entire morning and was followed by a formal lunch at which senior managers were invited, in addition to a few local management representatives such as myself.

There I was sitting next to the CFO of the parent company whom I had never met and among a number of subsidiaries, directors and executives. Quite frankly, it was intimidating and very difficult to strike up conversation with such senior executives. The atmosphere did not stop a number of managers from putting forward their views and ideas. It was obvious that they wanted to make an impression, as I did, but I was too uncomfortable and shy to interject and talk over the conversations.

Interest Creates Conversation

I only knew one very senior executive on the board, the CFO of the subsidiary I worked in, who had undertaken one of my interviews. He had interviewed me prior to my formal appointment, at which time we discussed my BMW. I had purchased a new BMW 320, which I found out soon after purchase had faulty paint. At the time of my interview I was involved in a protracted warranty claim with BMW Australia. I wanted the car replaced; they wanted to repaint it.

The subsidiary CFO, seeing I was not in the conversation, asked from the other end of the table 'Tell me John, how did you go, with your warranty claim?'

The noise fell away as I responded. 'Funny you should ask – they finally agreed today to give me a new car.'

'Unbelievable!' he exclaimed. 'I've never heard of a car company replacing a car under warranty, well done!!'

The parent company's Finance Director asked, 'What type of car?'

'A BMW 320,' I answered.

'My God,' he said and turned to the group parent company CEO. 'You couldn't even get your 7 Series replaced after it just stopped several times.'

The Group CEO replied, 'And your Range Rover has also been a real issue.'

The rest of lunch was spent discussing my experience along with everyone else's, and how I managed to get my car replaced.

It is amazing how one common connection and an interest in the subject led to the discussion being dominated by my experience!

Been There Done That

I was now working for a significant Australian publicly listed business and the subsidiary my division was part of was a star performer, specialising in container packaging: this is packaging that ends up on the shelf.

The division I worked in comprised seventeen once privately owned folding carton plants, purchased in a series of acquisitions to form the country's second largest folding carton operation in Australia. The private folding carton businesses purchased were absorbed into a conglomerate and burdened with overheads, which required higher volumes, so the business found itself competing on price without a coherent strategy. The division was a strategic group purchase to deal with the recycled cardboard produced by a massive plant in Queensland.

Because it was consumer packaging it was put under the container packaging arm, which included flexible (wrappers), closures (caps), cans (metal and aluminium cans), sacks (cement and milk powder bags), etc. That was where the similarities ended, as most container operators were dominant or duopolies with significant market share. Folding cartons had only a minority market share and was second behind the leader, which had only a marginally higher market share. That left hundreds of independents with the majority of the market, including niche specialists (fragrance, pharmacy, etc.) and general printers with lower overheads and who produced simple products like Wendy's ice cream holders or McDonald's fries' cups.

The folding carton division was expected to use recycled cardboards that were inferior to the virgin cardboards used by its largest competitor. Recycled cardboards have shorter fibre lengths than virgin boards, which are made from trees. Folding cartons are called folding as they are shipped folded flat, already glued on one side and with heat sensitive glue applied to the out folded flaps. Customers' packaging machines push the cartons open, insert the product (biscuits, cereals, lollies), push the flaps closed and apply heat – all at astonishing speed. They didn't like recycled cardboards as the quality was often variable, and if one of the boxes didn't open when it should, the entire production line stopped. The boxes required much thicker cardboard, too, which added to the price.

Empathy Creates Trust

It was not long before I was given the first national tender to prepare. Thrown to me, the request for tenders (RFT) specified numerous requirements that the division was not equipped to deliver. The customer, the country's largest biscuit manufacturer, provided considerable volume growth, and two of the folding carton division's seventeen plants supplied the company. If the tender was successful, seven plants would be needed to supply the customer; if unsuccessful, the two currently supplying it would need to close.

The general manager of the division was not sensitive to the overall requirements of the RFT, which required the tenders to satisfy a wide range of 'Global Supply Partnership' requirements in procurement circles. At the time, globally competitive pricing and practices were emerging as key elements of supply agreements. In our first briefing to discuss the approach he wrote something on the top of the page on his pad, ripped it off, folded it in half and handed it to me so I couldn't read what he had written. I asked what it was and he told me to open it, so I did – written were the words 'PRICE, PRICE, PRICE, and PRICE'.

At least we had consensus that we understood what the customer's primary objective was – globally competitive pricing. What we had to identify was what that price needed to be and what they **NEEDED** to do to obtain it.

I remember reflecting on the division between the management and the unions when the same guys were operating printers and cutters worth literally millions of dollars, and were critical to controlling quality and waste. I knew from my dyeing and finishing days that these people were the secret to unlocking enormous profitability. Two other things I took away from my textile industry days were that you had to be strategic (they were the only accredited dye house – this was the only recycled cardboard available in Australia) and the customer was always right (you had to deliver on price without jeopardising quality or service).

You Have to Meet the Need

So, if it was price, we had to provide the best price with a number of strategic hooks. To determine the best volume mixes we spoke to the shop floor. We obtained their trust by explaining what the consequences of winning or losing the tender would be. We **ASKED** questions, **LISTENED** to their answers and sought to **UNDERSTAND** deeper issues that they had. Would they hold off breaks to allow the presses to run if the jobs ran longer? How long could a press actually run with the same job before it needed to stop? How long would it take to print the most popular product if we made a month's supply in one plant at the one time? And on it went. To determine the medium- to longer-term requirements, we spoke to the parent company, to the cardboard plant and to the customer and **ASKED** what their strategic objectives were.

Our parent company believed in recycling and saw it as a competitive advantage in cardboard packaging.

The customer saw globally competitive pricing as critical to the survival of their manufacturing plants. Being part of an international food manufacturer, their biscuits could be made in a wide range of countries. We asked many questions, listened, and respected each stakeholder's position and desired outcomes.

What we ended up presenting was a compelling tender document that proposed very competitive pricing for national volumes and national forecast commitments. That enabled the business I worked for to manufacture the cartons in the factories that best suited us in volumes that reduced the cost of manufacturing substantially. We also proposed a program to promote the recycled cardboard with an emblem that the customer could display on their cartons. That would appeal to consumers and which was something our competitors could not do.

Four weeks later we were advised that we had won the tender. No revisits for further information on pricing, no playing one bidder off against the other, and straight into changeover. A simple phone call followed by a letter. Unbelievable! This was the start of the reverse of the previous three years' steady volume decline for the folding cartons division.

As I interfaced with the biscuit manufacturer and other major customers I became increasingly interested in fast moving consumer goods (FMCG) and decided to enrol in a Masters in Marketing. I didn't like being pigeonholed as an 'accountant', and while clients accepted commercial acumen, I was still an accountant to the business I worked for.

Perception is Reality

The marketing qualification changed a number of people's perceptions of me, particularly those of external parties, who approached me to go over to a major footwear company just as I was being accepted into the general management program which commenced with plant management responsibilities.

I did not fancy moving interstate to run plants and the approach to join the footwear business had me back at the right level again, as the finance director overseeing marketing. In addition, the business had moved its head office from Adelaide to Melbourne. Both the finance director and sales and marketing director declined to relocate, so my new the job required skills across both disciplines as the roles were transitioned.

The business was part of a British company that had been owned and controlled by descendants of the original brothers. Locally it was a large business employing some 2000 people. The company operated a very vertical business from shoe components, the manufacture and importation of shoes, wholesale distribution and some retail representation. The majority of employees were involved in manufacture, which had a bleak future. With the removal of quotas just before I started and the reduction of tariffs, the business was extremely vulnerable and faced the prospect of significant losses over coming years.

Faced with a tumultuous job and needing to establish new head office functions, I approached one of the accountants I had employed at the business forms business some years earlier.

We Back People Not Roles

When I tracked him down he had left the company after a falling out with another new CEO, had separated from his wife, and was at rock bottom. I convinced him to contract to the business I worked for and help me, and I gave him enormous flexibility while he got his life back together.

You Are Treated Differently at the Top

I quite quickly took over as CEO following the departure of the incumbent who had a falling out with a new global CEO. The new global CEO was young and successful, and had a mandate to initial public offering (IPO – float it on the stock exchange) the group in the UK. That saw me promote the two accountants I had employed into directorships, and a hectic pace of change ensued as we tried to move production offshore while retaining and expanding our wholesale and retail presence.

The appointment to CEO was quite unexpected and sudden, and within one or two weeks I was inundated with approaches from all sorts of organisations and people. One, which was taken rather seriously, was the approach from an executive search firm (head-hunters), who invited me to a round table lunch for new CEOs. On the highest level of the Rialto, with outstanding views of Melbourne, the lunch was round table silver service. There were seven of us (new CEOs) and seven of them (head-hunters). There was trepidation, knowing why we were there and why they wanted us there.

They wanted the new CEOs to use their services, as often a new CEO will fill many senior roles with new appointments. As new CEOs we were there because we knew our next jobs would come from the head hunters. Let's just say it was an environment based on **MUTUAL RESPECT**!

The topic of the lunch was 'What is it like as a new CEO?' One by one the new CEOs explained the responsibility, the daunting objectives, the pressure and the necessity to keep an eye on detail while navigating a huge ship. Most of the comments were more or less the same. Finally it was my turn, but we were running out of time. The chairman said politely, 'John, given the familiar theme we have already heard, would you mind keeping your experiences brief?'

I replied, 'Not at all. I will be brief as, unlike the other guests, I was promoted from CFO to CEO overnight, and I have noticed two distinct changes.'

The chairman politely asked what the changes were. I explained the first was that the accountants didn't invite me out for a beer any more on Friday nights. Everyone laughed, particularly the head-hunters. The second was that everyone now laughed at my jokes and quite frankly, I was never that funny. The room was in fits of laughter.

These two things taught me a valuable lesson: not every representation is entirely truthful, particularly when you are in a genuine position of influence.

Commitment Does Not Guarantee Security

Despite working harder than ever before and making some serious progress navigating our way out of local manufacturing, the overall returns constantly fell short of the parent company's expectations. To put this in perspective, the parent company in the UK had no sources of supply from China and could offer us no genuine support to develop offshore manufacturing, yet they expected little old Australia, with the small volumes we sold (relative to the European and US markets), to source profitably from offshore.

We resorted to construction in Fiji and started to develop another international brand, which was the largest volume brand we manufactured and distributed, and also the most profitable. This brand was owned by a US based manufacturer, wholesaler and distributor of general-purpose footwear, which was rapidly outselling our parent company's brand on a global basis. We had an unbelievably good licence agreement too, which could not be broken, and saw us paying an extremely low royalty per pair sold. The US licensor had made significant inroads into China, so we piggy-backed on their volumes, securing very good pricing in addition to the respect of the Chinese factories, which saw Australia as an extension of their relationship with the US company. Being the social animals that we Australians are, it was not difficult to maintain that **FAÇADE**, and as a result we were treated extremely well and rarely experienced the supply or quality problems that plagued the local industry as it ventured into importing from China.

Despite an evergreen licence at a ridiculously low royalty rate, our parent company decided they could no longer support a competitor's brand and decided to withdraw from the Australian and New Zealand markets. I was blind-sided. I didn't agree with that decision so obviously was not invited to stay on to carry it out, and I found myself on the market for the second time in my life.

What made this event a little different, though, was the manner in which the strategy was implemented. Rather than wind it down straight away and inform the local management, the **FAÇADE** was maintained that it was business as usual, while licence agreements were negotiated behind the local management's back.

One of the accountants whom I had employed and promoted to Operations Director was appointed as an interim CEO while a new CEO was secured.

Respect is Not Always Mutual

The management team was understandably concerned for their own futures and blamed everything they could on the previous CEO – me!!! Despite my representations that the business was going to be closed they carried on as if they had wonderful careers, and the interim CEO put his hat in the ring for my job. This was never going to happen according to my assessment of the situation.

I tried to explain what I thought would play out but did not force my views too harshly as it just sounded like sour grapes. They chose not to **LISTEN** or to **UNDERSTAND** what was evolving from my perspective.

I really did **UNDERSTAND** their desire to secure their roles, I had

EMPATHY for them and held no animosity. I was later quite pivotal as a referee for a number of them as they secured new roles with the inevitable closure of the business.

One reference was for the Operations Director for a CEO role with a finance company. The departing CEO was moving to the international head office. He knew the Operations Director from a previous role and was considering putting him forward as a candidate. Before he did this he had canvassed my thoughts quite early in his evaluation process.

A Rare Look Behind the Façade

I really would rather look to the good side of people, as opposed to the bad, and that allowed me not to hold grudges, to have genuine **EMPATHY** by trying to rationalise behaviour and the reasons for it, and to give many, many people the benefit of doubt. This meant second, third and often fourth chances, particularly when I respected their technical and professional capability.

The ability to genuinely **EMPATHISE**, rather than react emotionally, allowed me to observe what appeared on the surface to be genuine representations. It was not until I had observed the same representations and knew the motives and facts that were apparent below or behind the scenes, that I realised the power of giving people a lot of rope. Nothing confirms your assessment is accurate more than finding out, when you genuinely need help and reach out to the people you know the best and whom you trust, and who you think will help you the most, that these are the people who quite possibly may help you the least.

Friends Rarely Directly Help

This is what happened to me when I turned to the search firms, ex-bosses like the ex-CFO of the business forms company, and the myriad of capable employees such as my Operations Director. Most didn't help at all, but maintained the **FAÇADE** of respect, expressed the desire to help while doing nothing, and in some cases were actually destructive in their interpretations of the past (my Operations Director in particular, as I found out). What really amazed me, however, was that these same people unashamedly looked for assistance and help when they wanted something: here are two examples.

Reciprocity is Rare

The CFO I initially reported to at the business forms company had returned to North America and the local business was finally delisted with the parent company's purchase of the remaining minority shareholdings. The lack of strategic focus had reduced a once mighty business to one sick puppy, and eventually the last management team found venture capital backers and started to negotiate a management buyout. The CFO whom I had reported to was the seller's representative and eventually a deal was agreed in principle.

The VC firm, however, lost confidence in the local CEO and called the deal off. The previous CFO responded by flying to Australia to try to restart negotiations. He went on to negotiate the deal with himself as the CEO and soon was back as CEO, with a considerable amount of leveraged equity. When he settled back permanently he did nothing other than reduce costs and progressively strip all the parent company royalties, fees and proprietary products, delivering immediate, substantial lifts in profits. He did this extremely well, with the right team around him and with steady steel and resolve.

After two years he orchestrated the exit of the VCs and himself through another management buyout, and became a multimillionaire for his efforts. He kept in touch throughout this journey, always ready to play golf as my guest, and this continued after he retired and returned to North America. In fact, a few of us were regularly contacted in advance of his return for the use of spare cars, for catch-ups and the odd round of golf.

It wasn't until I started the firm that I now run that I understood the true **RELATIONSHIP**. With no clients, no income, a new child on the way and a significant investment in the start-up of the firm, I met my former boss over a round of golf as my guest. I was genuinely hoping to be referred into a new list of his contacts in Australia to leverage my lead flow. He knew a number of influential people, particularly in the CEO networks and the venture capital markets. I had identified him as being potentially useful to me, just like I later observed new partners grading their networks.

At the end of the round I really could not get a word in. He did not want to find out how I was going or if he could help me. I was poised to **ASK** for some referrals as soon as the conversation lent itself to the subject, but to my surprise the only outcome was his expressed desire for me to find him Australian non-executive directorships he could hold between his commutes back and forth from North America.

I really think he thought he was helping me by displaying confidence that the firm I had just started could help him. I only met him once more after that. And lo and behold he did in fact help me, it just took a few years for me to see it as clearly as I now do.

Reciprocity Flushes Out Mutual Respect

My former Operations Director from the footwear company never purposefully made contact with me after I left, although we bumped into each other occasionally and met from time to time at social events where there were mutual friendships and connections. As a result, I was disappointed with him and doubted his sincerity as a friend.

When the CEO of the finance company's mother died, I thought should I let my former Operations Director know that his Jewish mother had died, and if you didn't turn up to a Jewish funeral you were generally not considered that close. Albeit with some hesitation, but knowing it was the right thing to do, I telephoned him and informed him of the death and funeral of our mutual friend's mother.

There he was at our friend's moment of personal hardship and grief, showing his support and respect, as in fact I was as well.

We Do Not Mind Asking for Favours

About a month later I was phoned by my former Operations Director to ask if I would be a referee. I agreed to do this and asked him to stay in touch if he got the job, as he would be working over the road from our new office.

He did get the job but never came over or even telephoned to advise me of the appointment. In fact, the first time I bumped into him in the coffee shop under our building he cornered me and slandered the previous CEO in relation to an alleged car rort by employees, which he claimed was endemic and constituted tax avoidance. He also criticised a sporting sponsorship, claiming the former CEO signed off before contract details were documented, resulting in major costs to the company. And on it went. While this didn't surprise me, a report by another professional colleague and friend some months later did reveal the world is indeed a small place.

We Are All Connected

My friend was a member of the CEO Forum, a group of CEOs of overseas-owned subsidiaries in Australia. It was quite prestigious, and a great networking venue that your current employer paid for. As the new CEO of the finance company, which was owned by an overseas parent company, my former Operations Director was eligible to join, which he duly did. He was sponsored by a recruitment executive for whom he worked in an interim capacity. I then referred him and vouched for him when he was made redundant from the footwear company.

At his introduction to the CEO Forum he was asked to introduce himself to a large forum, as was customary. So he addressed a room of some 100 CEOs and their guests and gave an outline of his career. This included the claim that he turned around the footwear company as CEO, taking it from 2000 employees and losing several million dollars to a small wholesaler and distributor of no more than sixty people making several million dollars – before moving on after successfully licensing the business to a large locally owned footwear distributor. He went on to embellish how poorly the footwear business was run before he took over.

The Truth Will Be Found Out

My friend, knowing my background, could not believe what he was hearing, but decided against a challenge in that forum. He obtained a copy of the slideshow and asked me a week or so later to re-explain what transpired while I was at the footwear company. Not only could his representation be extremely damaging to my reputation, it was factually incorrect.

He had been the CEO of the footwear business, but only in an interim capacity and only for three weeks. A new CEO was appointed almost immediately after I left. He stayed on as the Operations Director and was instructed by the UK to close all manufacturing, after which he was made redundant.

To the few people at the event that did know me, his portrayal of his role at the footwear company did more harm to his reputation than it did to mine. It is a small world and your truth will be found out as David Penglase, author of *Intentionomics* would attest.

You may rationalise that such disloyalty is an individual characteristic, and no doubt there is some truth to this; but what I observed over a long period of employment was that there is often a lack of **MUTUAL RESPECT**.

It became clear that there were a myriad of situations where people did not value their relationship with people in the same way as those people did with them. The easy interpretation is scepticism, and self-interest, but what I learned was that it went far deeper than this. They maintained a **FAÇADE** of friendship out of convenience or value to them, but their intention did not correlate with their **FAÇADE**.

Giving nothing to a friendship and receiving nothing from it (other than pleasantries) is not a relationship based on mutual respect – and you soon find this out when you start looking for help from the people you know the best.

Another Referral

Immediately after the footwear business I was introduced to another once formidable packaging company. It was a large conglomerate of mainly packaging businesses and one of Australia's first notable management buyouts that was backed by venture capital.

While I was at the previous packaging company, the parent company had acquired the group and integrated their packaging businesses into their own operations. In fact I helped integrate a few of the businesses, the largest being the cigarette carton business. The non-packaging business was retained under the group name and comprised an innumerable quantity of security printing and personalisation businesses. Chequebooks, driver's licences and credit cards were the major areas, and extremely profitable, with earnings before interest and tax (EBITDA) of some $35 million on turnover of $85 million.

Not being industry experts, the packaging group found the changing dynamics of the security printing industry quite different to their core business and decided to sell the remaining pieces of the business.

Electronic printing was emerging, as was smartcard technology. Electronic payment processing was growing rapidly and chequebooks were believed to have no future (paperless office paranoia again!); the future capital upgrade requirements were significant. So the business was sold into a US card solutions business operating in similar areas in North American markets. The purchasers paid $110 million, put $5 million down and borrowed $105 million from a syndicate of mainly foreign investment banks. They then instructed the local management to grow the business at any cost, which they proceeded to do. There were really only two or three major pieces of business available as the banks outsourced their traditional in-house chequebook and credit card manufacture.

They won everything they went for on price, without strategic hooks to creep back value-adds. What a disaster! Revenue grew to $130 million and EBITDA fell to $7 million in as little as two years. Not even interest could be met, and the business was in serious default with its bankers. The parent, fearing receivership, sought help; and an interim management firm was asked to find an interim CEO to manage the break-up and sale of the business.

At some point in that break-up and sale process, my name came up through a friend (another referral) who worked at the company, as a possible commercial person to be contracted to restore financial credibility with the banking syndicate.

It is Never How it Appears at Face Value

I quickly learned that the cheque business, which they were trying to sell, actually generated all the cash. Contrary to popular paranoia, volumes were not falling they just weren't growing. The growth areas, credit cards and smartcards, were capital intensive and very low margin, and sucked up all the cash. Furthermore, there was no real strategic focus, and on my observation this was Australia's first secure electronic payment and procurement business. Every day the banks sent electronic data to the business of all the accounts that had used their trigger cheques. The business received the data in secure formats, decoded it, re-sorted it, validated it and then printed personalised cheques that they bound and mailed to the customers on the same day. Unbelievable!

So while they were trying to break the business up for scrap I could see an IPO on the back of the tech bubble! I and the small finance team quickly got on top of the reporting and once again, by talking to the operators, **ASKING OPEN QUESTIONS** and delving into our previously **UNKNOWN** knowledge of the business started to understand the cost and profit drivers. We were soon in a position to prove that the paper business should not be sold and that the growth areas of the business needed far tighter controls and restructuring. We also had to change sales emphasis, as electronic payment systems, gift cards and smartcards started emerging as the next wave of technologies and products.

Of course, the US parent company did not like the numbers being forecast, and there was no cash available to fund restructures or new equipment to improve those numbers.

The Truth Has to be Told

This had them resorting to the same old tactic of bullying local management into submitting unachievable forecasts. At my first presentation to the Americans I provided the realistic numbers. The global CEO (and major shareholder) went wild. He screamed and punched the table and emphasised that the banks would foreclose if shown those numbers. I explained that that was why we were looking at them first; to decide how to approach the situation and secure the funds needed to fix and then IPO the business.

He kept screaming and carrying on, although he became less vocal as time progressed. Eventually I said, 'Look, why don't you just write down the profit number you want from each area of the business on this pad?' I pushed a pad and pen over to him. 'Go on, just write them down so we can go off and support them but can you also please just date and sign them off as well so we can all sign as witnesses.'

The room was silent!! No one had ever stood up to the CEO before. They had always avoided confrontation, then criticised him behind his back.

The Truth Comes Out

What became clear over the next several hours as the **FAÇADES** of both businesses were removed, was that the US parent had no other money, and was in financial difficulties itself. The only viable option, to restore profitability and the underlying value of the business, was to ask the banks for more money. This required us to present the actual and most likely position if we were to move forward if nothing was done, then present what we wanted to undertake, the cost of doing it and the returns expected to be derived.

This is in fact what happened, and the banks did inject further funds, but on a few important conditions: one was that I would become a director and CFO, which I considered a backward step. As a result of my reluctance to take up the appointment I negotiated hard with my contract, which included some free equity and which, could make me a lot of money if the business carried out what we said we could do.

Timing is Everything

Unfortunately for me, the US parent went into Chapter 11 (similar to receivership in Australia) in the US before the equity could be assigned. By the time a venture fund had emerged with control my equity entitlement was removed.

This gave me an excuse to sever my contract and start another chapter of my life.

I decided at this point that anything I did in the future needed to be within my boundaries of my control – so I started looking at acquiring a business – and that was the beginning of **nem**!

ABOUT THE AUTHOR

John S. McKinstry is founder and Managing Director of **nem** Australasia Pty Ltd, a management consulting firm specialising in assisting businesses to achieve their objectives far more quickly than they can achieve with their own resources.

As the Managing partner and keynote speaker, he has led a partner group that has assisted thousands of businesses and organisations, ranging from start-ups to multi nationals but with particular emphasis on assisting medium-sized private businesses that wish to grow.

To learn more about the services and skills of the firm please visit www.nem.net.au

DID YOU ENJOY THE BOOK?

Register on the **nem** mailing list at nem.net.au/animals and obtain access to a range of resource materials and a complimentary assessment that will determine how your business could benefit from the deployment of the VALUE Encounter Methodology.

Register at
nem.net.au/animals